Dimensions of Sustainability

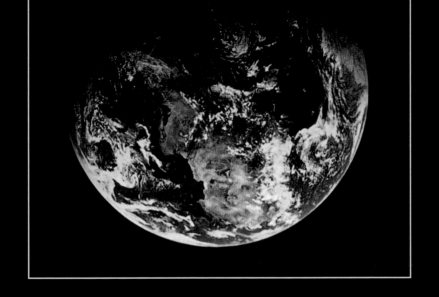

ARCHITECTURE   FORM   TECHNOLOGY   ENVIRONMENT   CULTURE

E & FN SPON
An Imprint of Routledge
London and New York

This edition published 1998
by E & FN Spon, an imprint of Routledge
11 New Fetter Lane, London EC4P 4EE

Simultaneously published in the USA and Canada
by Routledge
29 West 35th Street, New York, NY 10001

Text set by MIT in Microsoft Word 6.0
Images Formatted using Adobe Photoshop 4.0
Digitally produced using Quark Xpress 3.32

Printed in Hong Kong by
Tenon & Polert Colour Scanning Ltd

British Library Cataloguing in Publication Data
A catalogue record for this book is available
from the British Library

ISBN 0 419 23620 1

Contents

Acknowledgements

Editing and Design Andrew Scott

Production Assistance Min Jung Maing -
with additional support from Mamta Prakash, Paul
Kim, Jim Bruneau and Andrew Miller.

Editorial Assistance Nina Chen, Allen Tsai, Twig Gallemore, Andrew
Miller,

The Dimensions of Sustainability Symposium was
funded in part by the Alliance for Global
Sustainability at M.I.T. and the School of Architecture
and Planning.

Special thanks to Matthew O'Connell and Rebecca
Berry for their invaluable help in the organization of
the Dimensions of Sustainability Symposium at MIT
in November 1996.

Thanks to the Rocky Mountain Institute for
permission to reproduce Bill Browning's lecture,
previously published on their CD ROM Green
Developments.

**This book is dedicated to
Raoul, Loren and Joshua - and your future.**

Foreword

Nazli Choucri
Massachusetts Institutc of Technology
Cambridge, Massachusetts, U.S.A.

Despite differences in definitions, perspectives and priorities, sustainability remains a critical challenge for everyone. In general, the problem is this: traditional patterns of industrial and economic activities are no longer viable, but alternative models are not yet developed. The historical trajectory of the industrial West cannot serve as a model for the development of the industrializing countries, but it cannot be discarded entirely. Ecological systems are severely strained by the cumulative effects of past industrialization and can scarcely
support added strains due to future patterns of growth, but there are major uncertainties about *what* must be done and *how*. In short, the international community as a whole is involved in a global search for new modes of development, new designs for social interaction, and new technologies for meeting evolving needs, wants, and demands.

The common dilemma for us all is how best to manage the interconnections between ecological conditions and balances, on the one hand, and social needs and priorities, on the other. This book is a major contribution to new thinking on the built environment. For the rich, the problem is how to maintain reasonable consumption patterns and standard of living while reducing emissions and environmental degradation. For the poor, the problem is how to meet basic needs, transcend conditions of marginality, and improve the level of economic well being — all without creating the pollution that is so prevalent in industrial societies. Addressing this challenge by necessity means developing better ways of managing matters of shelter, infrastructure and built spaces, as well as improving modes of transforming natural habitats in forms consistent with social goals, priorities and purposes. The various conceptions of sustainable development — well over 50 at the last count — are rooted in the Brundtland Commission report defining the form of development as one of meeting the needs of future generations without foreclosing options for the future. This view serves a the essential starting point, to be sure, but it is hardly sufficient as an analytical guide or as a policy directive. Indeed, in many parts of the world the pressing priorities are shaped by the dual imperatives of survival and endurance.

Strategies for managing the built environment touch upon all the key dimensions of sustainability at all levels and in all contexts. These include: *ecological balance* (preserving the resilience of natural environments and balances); *economic performance* (enabling markets for generating production and consumption patterns); *institutional capacity* (meeting the organizational needs of private entities and firms and public agencies); and viable governance (ensuring effective policy, regulation, and accountability).

This book illustrates how the joint impact of innovation, adaptation, and evolution may yield creative and effective response strategies. It also helps show how such strategies may facilitate transitions toward sustainability. Written for specialists, this book has important messages for generalists. Targeted at professional architects and practitioners, it is also of relevance to planners in broader contexts. Addressing innovations in the field of architecture, it represents a concerned effort to meet the challenges of sustainability head-on in a domain that affects us all, namely built environment. In short, this book will be of great interest to individuals and institutions responsible for implementing new strategies toward sustainability — everywhere, and at all levels.

Andrew Scott
Massachusetts Institute of Technology

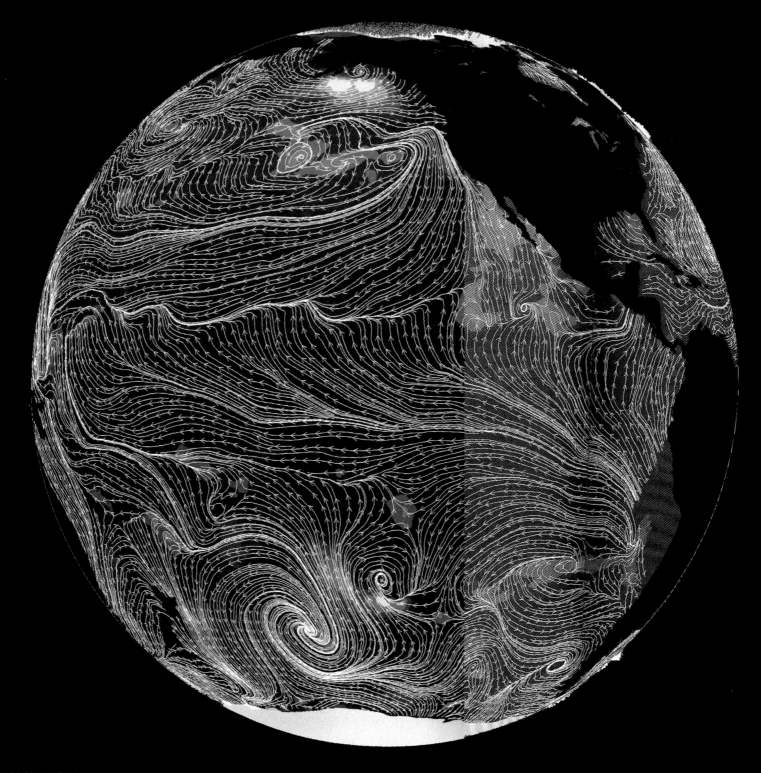

2.00 Mother Earth: the dynamic effect of wind patterns over the
Pacific

Introduction: A Time for Change and Innovation

Andrew Scott
Massachusetts Institute of Technology
Cambridge, Massachusetts, U.S.A.

2.01 Interior of a Ram Yantra, Delhi, India: a cylindrical instrument and construction for reading the sun's altitude.

It is a timely moment to set the context to our Symposium that took place in November of 1996. In recent weeks there has been the meeting of 163 nations at the Climate Conference in Kyoto in Japan trying to hammer out a global strategy to manage climate change and reduce carbon emissions. This followed the Special Session of 70 Heads of State at the United Nations in New York, the environmental Earth Summit which was a follow up to the conference in Rio de Janeiro 5 years earlier.

How have we fared? Not so well it transpires. The multi-national negotiations for the reduction of greenhouse gases have only served to illustrate the complexity of the scenario, in particular the difficulty of bringing developing countries on board while the industrial nations, and especially the US, still have to prove their interest in putting it on the agenda and their ability to get their own houses in order. One can feel some sympathy with those from developing countries that ask why they should be held to account when others have been so profligate and uncaring of energy consumption and natural resources'. While the months and years ahead will demonstrate whether such a climate treaty can be attained and then acted upon to seriously halt the greenhouse gas emissions and CO_2 build up, these recent discussions have served warning that ultimately the US in particular, has to tackle its profligate lifestyle, abundant use of energy and apparent public insularity against a recognition as the world's leading polluter.

A reduction of emissions, as proposed at Kyoto, to about 5% universally below 1990 levels and 8% below in the case of the US by the year 2010 or shortly after will be difficult to achieve, with or without the entrepreneurial effects of market forces and international trading of emissions quotas. For such progress to be made, major reductions in energy consumption and dependence on fossil fuels will need to take place although, as the experts point out with caution, this is only a fraction of the 60% reduction that some predict as necessary to reverse the climate crisis to ultimately "safe levels". No doubt, there will be very choppy political waters ahead for many years to come but at least one can be grateful that the issue of our shared environment is center stage. Architecturally, the necessity and opportunity for design and technological innovation has rarely been greater.

The United States boasts some 4% of the world population and yet currently generates some 23% of global carbon dioxide emissions, otherwise known as greenhouse gases. Fed by an economic boom that has overwhelmed steady improvements in energy efficiency, the United States now appears likely to increase CO_2 emissions by at least 13% this decade, thus reversing what it promised to do in Rio de Janeiro: a commitment to reduce greenhouse gas

2.02 detail from Delhi's Samrat Yantra, an equinoctial sundial, with steps winding like a system of cogs.

2.03 protective buffered microclimates formed by windscreens of pine trees in the open landscape of Shimane Prefecture, Western Japan.

output to the level of 1990 by the year 2000. The picture in Europe, where public awareness is far stronger, is generally more positive with Germany, Britain and Russia among others, having more success in responding to targets and to international treaties. The European Union is now proposing to cut emissions by 8% from 1990 levels by the year 2010.

The Rio conference led to the call for "sustainable development" (which has been defined and interpreted in a mulitude of ways ever since) with the definition of "paths of social and economic progress that meet the needs of the present without compromising the ability of future generations to meet their own needs".

What has this interpretation got to do with Architecture? What is the trickle down structure from political intention to architectural action? With this context in mind "sustainability" has become a familiar word but one that still creates a level of confusion and uncertainty. To many professionals and clients of buildings, it is far from clear how a broad concern for our environment translates into action at the level of design strategies and the particularities of Form. Added to this there is not an understanding of the connectivity of the "dimensions of sustainability", to the world of ideas at differing scales.

With this in mind, the symposium was established to overcome this disparate thinking and to broaden our

understanding of what being "sustainable" can become. What it actually becomes is not just an environmental strategy but a means of making buildings that are more user responsive, more humane places to inhabit, more intelligent in the way they balance their energy flows, more respectful of nature and the resources it offers, and more understanding of buildings having a life span during which they undergo substantial change and adaptation. Put together, it simply equates to better designed places in tune with the environment.

In so many ways it is also easier to define the "unsustainable" forms of practice from what should, or needs to be sustained, for so many "acts of building" appear to contradict the forces of nature. The act of building inevitably consumes resources, but in the act of construction or development we have to understand our actions as part of a larger system: one that has to work with the earth and its problems rather than working inspite of it. While there is the necessity to understand the performance characteristics of a project - the energy, the level of harmful emissions and the resources - the larger meaning lies in the ability to develop sustainable patterns and networks for living and working at many scales. Therefore it enhances the notion of a "cultural sustainability" of which the building becomes one cell in a larger ecological and cultural system: an understanding of the future viewed through the lens of the past and systems upon which we depend.

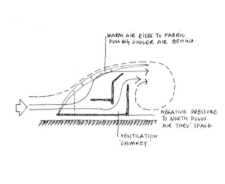

2.04 The Intelligent Pavillion: integrating photovoltaics and fabric structures. A competition won by Andrew Scott and Paul Donnelly.

2.05 the Intelligent Pavillion: sectional ideas for natural ventilation flow and PV integration.

At the heart of my concern and interest in being environmentally conscious is this question of the Form, founded upon a belief that if a certain agenda is absorbed into the design process, somewhere down the line it manifests itself in the formal composition of the building's physical and spatial parts.This might be the concept and typology, the urban form or be at the detailed level of technological components. For too long, being environmental has been seen as simply being energy efficient. While this approach is inherently admirable, to gain a broader base of acceptability the pillars of energy efficiency have to be related to other user gains and benefits. We need to understand and demonstrate the productivity and performance benefits deriving from sustainable environmental ideas and integrate these with the notion of 'life cycle' cost into economic formulations.

Energy has too often become the domain of either the engineer to tweak the mechanical system or its controls or become the domain of the techno-enthusiast to bolt on renewable technology without examining the larger role and form of the architecture. The "solar movement" fell into this cul-de-sac in the 1970s and the 80s, marginalising itself with an abundance of projects that may have been great energy savers or producers but represented minimal progress in integrating new renewable technologies into new paradigms for lwork and living. As a result of this compartmentalized form of thinking, the design professions are limited to a model of

buildings that is based largely upon modernist principles of both an abundant and invisible energy source and one where architects still assume little strategic responsibility for the control of the environmental systems as an integral part of a building's dynamic ecological system. We still continue to design structures that are totally unresponsive to their context through climate and orientation, that ignore and fail to harness natural forces, and which consume vast amounts of energy to enhance an unsustainable mode of working.

But there is significant hope. In 1990's we have begun to see a number of ambitious architectural projects that break this mold in buildings that reveal some innovative concepts for harnesssing light, natural ventilation, cooling and the generation of energy. This new generation of buildings point the way to forms that can elegantly use 50% less energy than current typologies and could eventually lead to the "zero energy" building supplying resources to the urban utility infrastructure.

However, the majority architects it seems still have limited interest in energy and the resource level of a building, let alone a more sophisticated understanding of environmental performance and assessment. Can we say that generally building design at the end of the century has reached a higher plain of technological, environmental and ecological integration ? Probably not. The concerns that have spurred

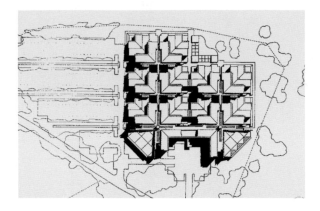

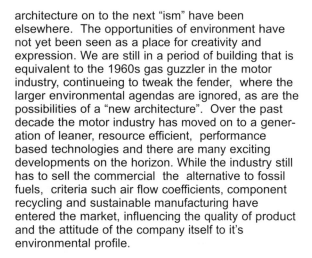

2.06 IBM low- enrgy office study: site plan showing the idea of the plan as a 'perforated carpet'

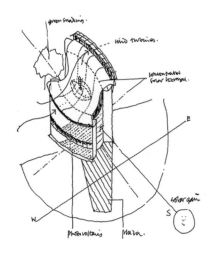

2.07 diagram for the zero energy autonomous building: Andrew Scott

architecture on to the next "ism" have been elsewhere. The opportunities of environment have not yet been seen as a place for creativity and expression. We are still in a period of building that is equivalent to the 1960s gas guzzler in the motor industry, continueing to tweak the fender, where the larger environmental agendas are ignored, as are the possibilities of a "new architecture". Over the past decade the motor industry has moved on to a gener-ation of leaner, resource efficient, performance based technologies and there are many exciting developments on the horizon. While the industry still has to sell the commercial the alternative to fossil fuels, criteria such air flow coefficients, component recycling and sustainable manufacturing have entered the market, influencing the quality of product and the attitude of the company itself to it's environmental profile.

As another example of this environmental account-ability and approach, Daimler-Benz in it's 1996 Environmental Report stresses it's continuing com-mittment to environmental protection through tech-niques which contribute to preserving and conserving natural resources. The report highlights it's develop-ment in hydrogen and air fuel cells, heat recovery 'heat wheels' in it's assembly hall, monitoring policies for air, water quality, energy and emissions, recycling electronic scrap, developments in biological oils, recycling of the modern bumper, the ecological basis of natural materials for the E-class vehicles, the 'fac-

tory of the future' being built near Stuttgart, and the ecological construction of the companies facilites in the new Potzdamer Platz in Berlin. One is clearly left with the impression of a company that understands the neccessity and benefit of environmental thinking to it's entire operation.

The original idea for the Dimensions of Sustainability symposium developed from a research database that we established at MIT of projects and technologies that conveyed clearly the role of design, and there-fore of the architect, in the technological and spatial form of a building. In doing so we predictably discov-ered a significant lack of precedents, especially in the United States, that demonstrated the role of design in developing credible alternatives for the non-domestic building to those that dominate our cities and urban horizons. It appears as a landscape of suburban sprawl dominated by millions of acres of heat absorbing flat roofs, mechanical penthouses pumping cooling energy into tinted glass faced build-ings with identical north and south facades, buildings where the lighting is never turned off, and yet build-ings that ask you (perversely) to use the revolving doors at the entrance in order to optimistically conserve energy.

Of those buildings we researched, many were of European extract, frequently spurred on by the research funding intervention from the European Commission. In the US, where environmental

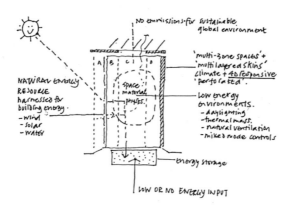

2.08 the diagram of new environmental technology: Andrew Scott

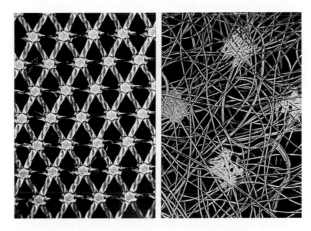

2.09 structures for man-made materials: new opportunities for degradability and recycling

regulation is still strenuously opposed in the name of free trade and market forces, tangible models were harder to find and existed more at the level of an ecological construction specification than in the realm of architectural strategies, concepts and user-led demands for better and more responsive working environments.

The Dimensions of Sustainability Symposium was therefore seen as a vehicle for expanding our potential definitions of what sustainability means, and to illustrate the way architecture can incorporate a meaningful and sophisticated understanding of environmental change and performance into design decisions. We were also interested in understanding how the cutting edge of computational design and simulation technology could support environmental ideas and decisions. So, we invited a group of individuals or practices that could demonstrate a track record in responding to "sustainability". We wanted to hear of their ideas and actions. We wanted a mix of disciplines, architects and engineers, educators and researchers that would typify the multi-disciplinary and collaborative framework of working that we believe is relevant to responding to today's needs. We were keen to see the innovative possibilities for "sustainability" in reinforcing the qualitative dimensions of architecture.

Through the focus of the symposium we explored and integrated these "Dimensions of Sustainability".

They concerned a range of topical issues at the cutting edge of architectural practice; ecology and evolution; real estate and the added value of green development; building typologies that harness natural light and passive ventilation; computer simulation of natural forces in a building form; digital technologies in establishing new, more sustainable patterns of work and industry; the necessity for basic human rights to an ecologically sustainable future; contemporary development at the cutting edge of engineering environmental design; resource efficient and ecologically degradable materials and structures; means by which we can understand building performance and flow as an integral part of understanding the forces in the longevity of a form; working communities and the need for sustainable and responsive infrastructures; and arguably most importantly, projects in practice that integrate conceptual ideas and design strategies with the act of making architecture and urban design, in this case the notions of micro-climatic envelope, bioclimatic form and ecological architecture.

I trust that this edited representation of the thoughts and work of those that came to speak at MIT creates a direction for architecture to move forward; to a genuinely environmentally responsive architecture in step with contemporary needs. It has to be a great opportunity to rethink what we do and how we do it.

William J. Mitchell
Massachusetts Institute of Technology

3.00 (top)&(below) The Learning Revolution- is not just computers in a classroom

Dematerialization, Demobilization, and Adaptation

William J. Mitchell
Massachusetts Institute of Technology
Cambridge, Massachusetts, U.S.A.

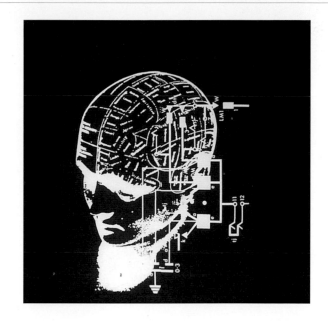

3.01 The microprocessor of human intelligence

I would like to begin this discussion by suggesting that many of the common ways of thinking about the issue of sustainability, and architectural responses to it, are not radical enough. Perhaps our assumptions and ideas need to be rethought — right back to their foundations.

Let me commence with the observation that, of course, local communities have always had to worry about responsible use of their resources. They have had to take care not to exceed the carrying capacities of their territories. In some cases — you can point out catastrophic ones like Easter Island, for example — local communities have failed to worry sufficiently about their local environments, and as a result have quite dramatically disappeared.

But our own era has developed a different perspective. We have had an increasingly urgent concern for global sustainability as well as the local variety. In other words, we have begun to worry about the finite carrying capacity for the Earth as a whole, and the fundamental need not to exceed that. That concern surely is a product of the age of transportation and telecommunications. Such global awareness could hardly have emerged without the shrinkage of distance that's been accomplished by sea and air travel over the last century or two. The telegraph, the telephone, radio, television, and now the Internet have had an even more powerful effect. For those of us who are old enough to remember, this global awareness was crystallized, some decades ago, by the arrival of the first extraordinary NASA pictures of the Earth as a blue sphere floating in space. It was a vivid, compelling image that nobody had ever seen before. And that was a transformative moment in our understanding of our relationship to our global habitat.

Then, as everybody knows, at the United Nations Earth Summit in Rio in 1992, the issue of global sustainability became the focus of international policy discussion on a very large scale. And the term sustainability - if it wasn't well established at that point - certainly became recognized as a signifier of what is, in fact, a very complex, multi-faceted, ongoing discourse. The scientists have their views of how issues of sustainability can be approached within a scientific framework; the engineers have a different perspective; my friends the economists have yet another perspective again. (Typically, the economists keep trying to explain to me that sustainability is an incoherent concept — that we don't really understand what we're trying to talk about. Indeed, I have to admit, they have some articulate arguments from their particular point of view.) The public policy people have another perspective again, as do urban planners.

As architects, our own specific contributions, of course, come in the domain at a midscale — in dealing with physical artifacts, and with the shape and

3.02 Traditional paper based book

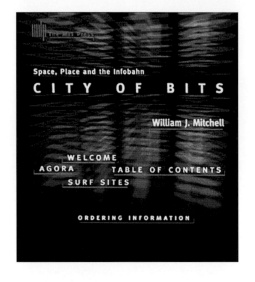

3.03 Electronic book

form that we give to our everyday environment. In the past, we have tried to respond sensitively to local and regional contexts; now we must deal with global concerns as well.

What, specifically I mean, do architects have to contribute to the discourse of sustainability - in both its local and global guises? I would like to suggest to you that — very often — architectural approaches to sustainability do not really get to the heart of the issue, and that we need to broaden our view if we're to make a contribution that really matters.

Let's consider the question of materials, for example. We very appropriately hear much about conservation, about recycling, about the use of environmentally appropriate materials, and about the use of building forms and urban patterns that are conservative of resources rather than wasteful. But what about radical dematerialization? What about satisfying human needs without construction? Or consider the question of transportation. This is often formulated as a question of how might you substitute pedestrian circulation or bicycle circulation or public transportation for the automobile. Fine! But once again, what about the possibility of large-scale demobilization? What about substitution, on a significant scale, of telecommunication for transportation? Let me expand on these points.

The very idea of dematerialization is often anathema

to architects because we have traditionally defined ourselves in terms of material responses to human needs. But there's another potential means available to us at this point. And that means is the use of information services, in particular contexts, instead of scarce material resources to serve human needs. And we can see this happening on a very significant scale at the moment. We're beginning to substitute bits for atoms. One example that has become very familiar to us all is the disappearance of the branch banks. With ATMs and electronic home banking you no longer need all that construction. You don't need all those branch bank buildings scattered around. You don't need to heat and cool them. And in fact, what we're seeing is these things being shut down in their thousands at the moment.

Then there are many potentials to separate information from material substrates such as paper. So, for example, a digital newspaper read on the screen does not consume newsprint. Of course you still may want to print some information; as everybody knows, computers have not made us paperless. But that printing can be highly selective to serve a temporary need rather than a long-term need, so that paper consumed can quickly go back into the recycling bin.

Notice that that kind of dematerialization has a double benefit. If you don't materialize things in the first place, not only does it economize on consumption of

3.04 Traditional branch banking

3.05 Electronic banking

resources, but it also decreases waste and pollution. If you don't produce a material good it never turns into waste that has to be managed. A used bit is not a pollutant.

So, in summary, there are now a great many possibilities for significantly reducing consumption of scarce material resources by employing electronic services in place of built facilities, and in place of material carriers of information. In the interest of sustainability we need to look very hard at the question of when you do really need to materialize things. We must focus our efforts on evaluating the materialize/dematerialize tradeoff very rigorously — always asking the question "Is there an alternative to materialization?" Is there a fundamentally different way to do these things?

Let us look at the issue of demobilization. In most large cities, as everybody knows, the inhabitants have to travel a great deal to get to work, to gain access to services, and to sustain social interactions. The costs in fuel, pollution, occupation of land by transportation infrastructure, vehicle manufacture and maintenance, and waste of time, are enormous. Frequently that problem has been exacerbated by planning approaches that have separated urban functions such as housing and recreation from heavy industry, and so on, to avoid creating unpleasant conditions and health problems.

Now, where access to work and services can increasingly be provided electronically, there is the possibility of significantly reducing those costs by partially substituting telecommunication for travel. One manifestation of that, dating from a number of years ago now, has been the widespread interest in telecommuting — which was originally sparked by the OPEC oil crisis. And we've probably only seen the tip of the iceberg on that issue, since the extent to which substitution can be effective depends on telecommunications bandwidth, and interface sophistication. Telecommuting by telephone, fax, and e-mail is very different from telecommuting supported by high-bandwidth digital telecommunications that provides things like teleconferencing, high-speed World Wide Web access, database access, and so on. As telecommuters get increased bandwidth, we're very likely to see significant growth in electronically supported working and service delivery.

But telecommuting, in fact, is a rather conservative idea — conceived of, typically, as the partial substitution of telecommunication for transportation within otherwise fairly stable urban structures. If you take the potentials of high-bandwidth digital telecommunication really seriously, though, you have to rethink basic ideas of the home and the neighborhood. What does it mean to reintegrate work and other activities into the home, for example? At the very least, it means more space, and more effective internal segregation of activities. That's a vital question if

3.06 Transportation infrastructure

3.07 Telecommunications infrastructure

we start to think about the future usefulness of the housing stock that we have, and the potential transformations of housing stock over the coming decades.

Or, take the question of what a neighborhood should be like. If you're going to spend most of your time there, it cannot just be a bedroom suburb. And certainly, electronically supported social islands — gated communities where privileged telecommuters closet themselves away — seem highly undesirable socially. So you need, for example, to take advantage of high daytime population in reconfigured, telecommuter-intense neighborhoods, and of reduced mobility, to support local services, and to create intense, diverse neighborhood life.

What makes an attractive neighborhood when traditional accessibility requirements weaken due to telecommunication? Where are the electronically relocatable likely to go? What are the appropriate uses of the greater locational freedom that this allows? These are basic questions in thinking about sustainability of urban patterns. So to summarize this one: demobilization is potentially a very effective and important strategy. But it is more complex than the simple notion of telecommuting. Finally, let me discuss the issue of intelligent adaptation. This is the use of intelligent systems, at various levels, to reduce waste by delivering just what's needed in a particular context, and no more. And a complemen-

tary strategy is to employ more responsive adjustment of prices and supplies for more effective demand management.

These sorts of strategies have become increasingly possible with the availability of inexpensive, ubiquitous computation. And less obviously, they have also been facilitated by recent great advances in sensor technology — so that you can now create systems that sense very effectively what's going on, and are able to respond to it. There are a number of different levels of this: from the product design level; through the architectural level; right up to the urban and regional level.

Now for example, you never read all the pages of a standard newspaper. On any given day, most of them are just wasted on you. But a personalized newspaper system may have a profile of your interests, and be able to use it selectively to print out just those articles that are of interest to you. That strategy consumes less paper to begin with, and produces less waste in the end. Take that to the level of transportation systems. If you buy a car, it sits in your garage most of the time. But contemplate a sophisticated, electronically managed automobile rental service — of the kind that several of the major automobile manufacturers have seriously been considering, and that has been looked at very hard in some European cities. A service of that kind might provide just the type of vehicle that you need just when you

3.08 Shopping mall of the past

FIDO: the Shopping Doggie!

by Continuum Software, Inc.

Con tinuum

Search Summary

The words in your product description appeared the following number of times: **digital**: 2869 products; **camera**: 296 products.

Good Doggie!

Fido found 43 products matching your product description. Happy shopping!

3.09 Shopping mall of the future

require it. But that only works if you have a sufficient level of highly sophisticated adaptive management of the system.

At the building scale, more intelligent control systems clearly can yield considerable savings. To take some obvious examples, consider, for instance, lighting systems that sense when anyone is around, and automatically adjust themselves according to occupancy. And there are a great many possibilities along these lines.

Even very large systems can benefit from more intelligent control. If electricity consumption can be varied intelligently at the user end, for example, then electric power utilities have the potential to motivate more thrifty and efficient use by introducing real-time electricity pricing, and similar strategies. At the level of transportation systems, if vehicles have transponders and road systems have sensors, then smart, electronically-adjustable road pricing, and parking pricing systems can be used to manage automobile transportation demand, and minimize traffic congestion.

So, in summary: the smarter control systems and strategies that the digital revolution makes possible have great potential for managing demand, for minimizing unnecessary consumption of resources in meeting demands, and for reducing generation of wastes and pollutants. If you look at some of the

work that is currently being done at The MIT Media Laboratory, one of the major thrusts is the "Things That Think" initiative — which is concerned with embedding sensing technology and intelligence in everyday physical artifacts. There's great potential here for developing Things That Think sustainably. So, there is a short survey of some of the more recently emergent means for dealing with issues of sustainability — ones that seem to me to be crucially important, but that don't fall within the traditional framework of what we take to be architecture. In addressing global sustainability, we should not be constrained by traditional disciplinary boundaries, or obsolete definitions of what are the proper scopes of our disciplines. What we need to do, as discussion unfolds, is to think broadly and adventurously. We need, in fact, to redefine our basic conceptions of what architecture is, and of what architects should be concerned about.

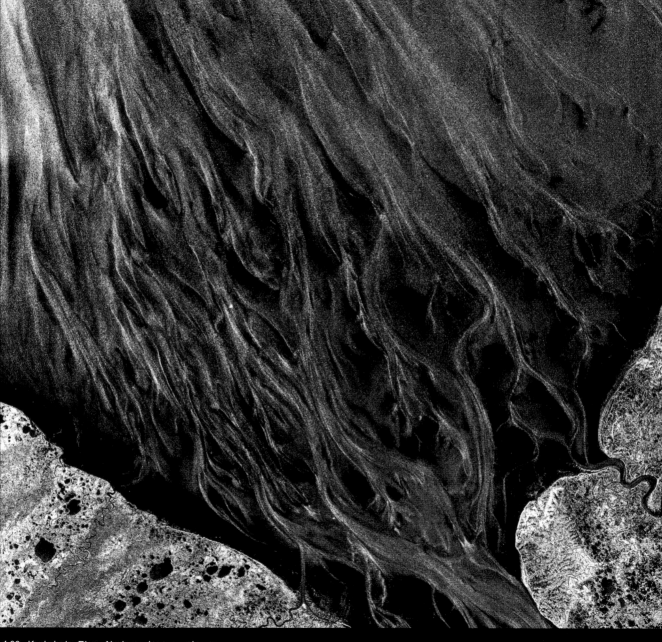

4.00 Kuskokwim River, Alaska: radar sensor image

Fitness, the Evolutionary Imperative

Ian McHarg
University of Pennsylvania
Philadelphia, Pennsylvania, U.S.A.

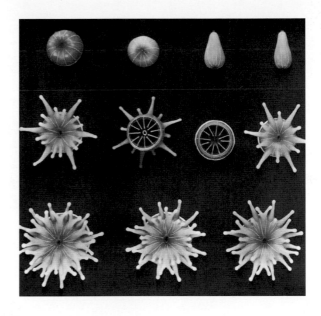

4.01 Transformation of coral polyps

I understand there's going to be something called Green Architecture. I've viewed this prospect with expectation for about forty years, and I've come to the conclusion that perhaps there will now be a green decade. I was at Harvard from 1946 to 1950, when it was dominated by Walter Gropius, Marcel Breuer, and others. Even then I began to have some apprehensions about the degree to which modern architecture was in fact going to save the world. And I had a fantasy. I close my eyes and I am in a room, and all the founders of modern architecture are there: BrunoTaut, Otto Wagner, Mies van der Rohe, Walter Gropius, Marcel Breuer, Jane Drew, Maxwell Fry, Philip Johnson. They are all discussing the prospect of changing the title of modern architecture to "the international style". This is discussed for a while. I stand up, and I say "You know, I'm only a student from Harvard." What less can you say? "I obviously have no authority. But as I listen to the discussions about transformation of architecture into the international style, I have to ask you if it is your intention to expunge all regional vernacular architecture and settlement? Because if it is not your intention, it may very well result".

Of course, during this period of time, no architects knew anything about the *environment*. I am not sure many know very much about it now. I have not yet been able to find a school of architecture anywhere on this continent, or any other, where architects are required to study "the environment". This is quite an extraordinary protestation. I was Chairman of Landscape Architecture at the University of Pennsylvania for 32 years. I decided that the architects who studied landscape architecture at the University of Pennsylvania had to know about the environment, and so I constructed a course. First of all, I bought a faculty of environmental scientists, and then I bought another faculty of ethnographers, cultural anthropologists and epidemiologists. We then devised a course at the irreducible minimum of meteorology, geology, geomorphology, physiography, hydrology, soil, plant ecology, animal ecology, ethnography, cultural anthropology, and computer science. And after a very difficult time - it took me about ten years to get these people to work together - which of course is antithetical to science and to government - we finally were able to offer an integrated view of "the environment" and "man in the environment".

We should address the antecedents of the conservation of environment in architecture. It really doesn't take very long. When I came to this country in 1946 only one person — one pair of persons really — were talking about the environment. They were the Olgyay brothers at Princeton, a very unlikely place, and they wrote about energy and architecture. And then along came James Marston Fitch, a wonderful man who wrote a book which really was preoccupied with the environment, particularly climatic regions. He got "House and Garden" magazine to

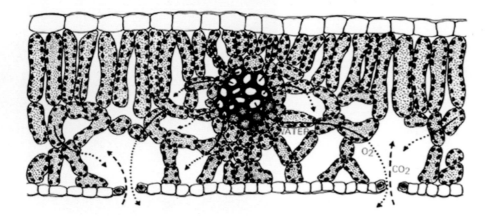

4.02 Structure of the section of a leaf to show oxygen, carbon doixide and water flow

produce handouts for each of the major ecological regions of the United States, with the appropriate climatic factors which he thought should be of interest for architecture. Of course this clearly had no effect at all. In comes Buckminster Fuller - a great wonderful man. The idea is that sailing ships are the best model for architecture. The modern legacy is very small, the Olgays, James Marston Fitch and Buckminster Fuller. But, of course the contribution of vernacular architecture is enormous.

So the question is what do I have to contribute to this scenario? Well, after I achieved this instant faculty that had this incredible concentration of highly opinionated, very skilled people - all of whom knew how to operate independently and didn't know how to operate cooperatively that I made my first discovery. The first thing I learned was in order to unify this group we had to have some unifying cause. There had to be a way by which all these disparate fragmented views of the environment were brought together as one, comprehensive, integrated view of the environment. I had to devise a method by which we could integrate them. And I discovered this wonderfully simple idea: *chronology*. That is, evolution is comprehensible through the operation of laws and time. So why don't we use time as a unifying device? So I said to all these people "Alright, who's got the oldest evidence around here?" A geologist stood up and said "My evidence is 500 million years old". I said "Start." So we would then talk about

geological history. And he said "You know, I can't do all this alone because the interaction of climate and geology makes geological evolution comprehensible." So I said "Alright, bring in the meteorologist. The pair of you proceed." So the two of them began to talk. The implications from the interaction of geology and climate is geomorphology. The form of the world as is comprehensible from the processes that have caused these forms to be vividly expressive. I said "Oh these data can be now reinterpreted to explain groundwater hydrology. The surfaces of surfacial and bedrock geology can be explained from geomorphology". And then soils, and then for plants, then for animals. And, if you go through the exercise in a clever way you can do this for man too. So the operation of chronology creates a layer cake. At the bottom bedrock geology, the next surfacial geology. Both of these reinterpreted as groundwater hydrology. The top surface, physiography. And then surfacial hydrology, soils, plants, animals, microclimate, mesoclimate, macroclimate. There we go. The question is now we've got a layer cake, and we've used chronology as a unifying device. Can we get a working model of it? I spent a few years of my life working on this thing. I even took it to the Institute for Advanced Studies, and these people were dumbfounded. They said "This man, you know, he plants bushes, where did he get this formulation?"

There's something called *syntropic fitness health*. It's probably one state where we have to use three

4.03 1930's midtown Manhatten: pollution and deprivation of the industrial city

words to describe it. Syntropic fitness state; syntropic fitness health. Then there's something called entropic misfit pathology disease. I mean, everybody ends up dead, but there is evolution, and life continues. There seems to be an oscillation by all systems to respond to these two poles.. Either creativity reflected in fitness and in health, as opposed then to randomness, disorder, degradation, misfit, and death.

The second law of thermodynamics says all energy is destined to be degraded. And then of course, the subject called entropy which Buckminster Fuller decided was a very, very bad term, which it is. And he said "Why don't we call it syntropy." Right? This is creativity. And he said "Let's look at this opposition. That is, scientists say that there were big bangs. And as a result of these explosions, instead of there only being an environment - cosmos consisting of hydrogen, helium - suddenly as a product of this incredible galactic explosion all the elements of the periodic table were created. Hydrogen, helium, lithium, beryllium, boron, carbon, oxygen, nitrogen, all the way up the periodic table. What a creative process this was. This is God at his best. "Start with a little hydrogen, helium and make the whole lot." Now, according to other physicists, not only did entropy increase dramatically as a result of that product, but there was a byproduct which was the creation of all the elements in the periodic table. This is a rather important point to make. That is, in every energetic transaction there will be an increase in

entropy. But in certain energetic transactions, while there will be an increase in entropy, there may be matter raised to a higher level of order than that which preceded it. This is creativity at a very, very profound level. Let's call it syntropy or creativity. So we have entropy and we have syntropy. The next term is fitness. Fitness has two meanings.

Charles Darwin said "The surviving organism is fit for the environment." Nobody has contradicted him for a hundred years. But Lawrence G. Henderson, a man who never made full professor at Harvard, said "Darwin is right but insufficient." The fact of the matter is there are an infinitude of environments, there are an infinitude of organisms, and there is a requirement for every organism or any system to find the fittest of all available environments, to adapt that environment, and to adapt itself to accomplish a better fitting. And there will always be a need for improving the fitting because the organism modifies the environment, and some environments then change and evolve too. So then the question is: what constitutes a fit environment? Henderson, wrote a wonderful book called The Fitness of the Environment in which he examined oxygen, hydrogen, carbon, nitrogen, seawater. He said "A fit environment could be defined as one where the largest parts of the needs of the consumer are provided by the environment as it is." And so then a fit environment is a least-work solution. To find the fittest environment where the largest things that you need are

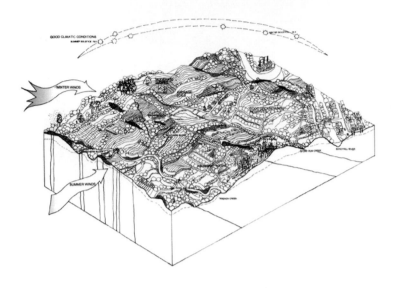

4.04 Natural features and settlemnt patterns: LARP studio University of Pennsylvania 1993

provided in the environment as found, means that you have to do less work of adaptation to satisfy your needs than any competitor. Therein comes Darwin saying "The surviving organism is fit for the environment."

So the question is do we have then a diagnostic view that allows us to see the degree to which syntropic fitting has been accomplished, and entropic misfitting has been accomplished. It's called *health*. If we use this concept, of course, at the level of billions of years, we say to the algae "Have you been able to find appropriate environments and adapt these to yourself?" The algae would say "You're right. I sure as hell have. Nobody's done it better." And if you move down to reptiles and birds, and so on, the time-scale changes, but the question doesn't. And those creatures who've been around for a hundred million years would say "Yes. We have been able to find fit environments, and adapt these environments really quite successfully." And if you move it down to a million years we've got man, and they too could say exactly the same thing. But if you want to now apply it to living creatures the same question would not be billions of years, millions of years, and so on, it would be now, and the question would be health. Are you *healthy*?

Two definitions of health. The World Health Organization defines the presence of health as being owned by people able to "seek and solve problems".

And there's a standby definition of health as the ability to recover from "insult or assault". Back to Darwin and Henderson — the ability to seek and solve problems. No reference now to muscles. So there could be a little man with bad teeth, dandruff, and there'd be another man from the Philadelphia Eagles - 300 pounds. And the question is "Who's healthy?" He has tens of thousands of employees, and so on. And this other fellow, this lump of narcissus, absolutely, totally ossified is of course clearly unfit. And so fitness is revealed by the little brown-toothed, balding old man. A very good definition, do we agree? If you find health, you have found organisms — for many levels. Cell, tissue, organism, ecosystem. You've found each system that has been able to find the most fit of all available environments, has been able to adapt that environment, and adapt the self to accomplish the most creative fitting. Therein lies success.

Now to confront the next question. I have a method. The method is you array all the layers of the environment chronologically, and you look down at every single cell, and you can see causality. And of course you can ask it questions. Where's a good place to build a new town? Woodlands. Where's a good place to build a new capital of Nigeria? Abuja. I have answered a lot of questions of this sort in my life, and the method is very simple. I array all the information about the environment in this causal way. And then I use my syntropic fitness health as

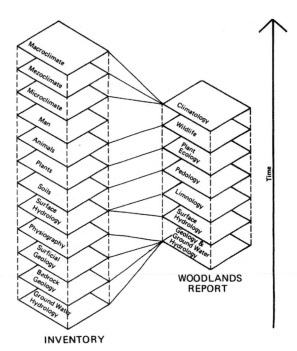

INVENTORY

4.05 Layer cake representation of the phenomena of landscape and cultural processes

Ian McHarg
University of Pennsylvania

criteria. And the next question I ask in this continuing education; are there attributes of fitness and misfit? Well yes. If you look over evolutionary time you'll see the progression has gone from simplicity to complexity. Why don't we look at single systems that move from simplicity to complexity. From uniformity to diversity. From instability to dynamic equilibrium. From a low number of species or parts to a higher number. To a low number of symbioses to a higher number. In turn, of course, from entropy to syntropy. So now, it's very clear the problem we all confront is called *adaptation*. And indeed if one said "Looking at all the things that man does, which of his professional activities most closely corresponds to the Darwinian Hendersonian challenge?" (That is, find the fittest environment, adapt the environment, and adapt the self.) Probably the best and most direct response is called planning and design. Now we know that architecture, landscape and planning at the moment do not correspond to this Darwinian Hendersonian imperative. I think they should. Then we have to recognize we're engaged in *adaptation*. What are the main instrumentalities by which adaptation's accomplished? The first one is physiological adaptation through mutation and natural selection. The great instrument found by Darwin. What an incredible man. Physiological adaptation by mutation and natural selection is not consciously used except with royalty. I mean, I don't think any of you have ever asked about, for example, the ancestors of your prospective spouse. You don't want to find out about

the father, grandfather, great-grandfather, and so on. Well you know, you fall in love with a woman, you know, I'm on my knees, I'm cutting up my heart, prepared to offer this palpitating organ. But with royalty that's not the way it happens. They do investigate the genealogy, and they're engaged in selective breeding for human beings. Which, as you know, has not produced handsomeness, has not produced beauty, has not produced intelligence, has not produced courage. Its only product is hemophilia. So, as you can see, it may be good for sweet peas, and corn, and cattle, and so on. But none of us use it. It's obviously not the most useful device for responding to adaptation by selective breeding. The next one is *behavioral adaptation*. And we're talking now about innate behavior. This is supposed to be only used by animals, it's not used by plants. Although we may be surprised.

So the last one is *cultural adaptation,* which includes language, and philosophy, and economics, and so on. And presumably, that is the most plastic of all the available kinds of adaptation, and I think probably the most suitable one. And I've already given away my punchline. That is if Darwin and Henderson's imperative were applied to this concept of adaptation, they would say that planning and design really are the appropriate responses. In which case then, I would suggest that the teaching of planning and design really have got to be formulated in terms of evolutionary biology, in terms of ecology,

SUITABILITY CRITERIA: RECREATION AND URBANIZATION

Development Type

Suitability Factor

Cost-Savings for:

Maximum Desirability for:

	FOUND-ATIONS			MAINT-ENANCE					WATER SUPPLY			LOCATION									ACTIVITY				

Column headers (vertical): Paved Surfaces, Light Structures, Heavy Structures, Site Drainage, Paved Surfaces, Lawns, Playgrounds, etc., On-Site Sewage Disposal, Domestic Use, Industrial Use, Irrigational Use, Favorable Microclimate, Topographic Interest, Long Views, Sense of Enclosure, Water-related Views, Vegetation Diversity, Wildlife Diversity, Historic Association, Educational, Fishing, Swimming, Canoeing, Boating

URBANIZATION

Rural Urban

Suburban

Clustered Suburban

Urban

RECREATION

Intensive

General

Natural

Cultural and Historic

Water-Related

Legend:

■ Critical ● Preferred/Compatible

● Optional ● Preferred/Partially Compatible

○ Desirable ○ Desirable

4.06 Suitability criteria for recreatiuon and urbanization in Medford Township, New Jersey, 1974

and physics. In terms of environmental planning, the one area which it seems to me we are dealing with very badly is hazards to life and health. The hundreds of thousands of people who are killed by drought, by earthquakes, by volcanoes, by tsunamis, by typhoons, by tornadoes, by floods is absolutely incredible. The amount of value of damages from this succession of hurricanes we had on the eastern seaboard of the United States recently, and the costs of insurance are unbelievable. It seems to me outrageous that we do not include these areas where there's a serious hazard to life and health as a consideration of planning. We should be able to use our information about environments in order to be able to ask questions. Where can you do what? Where shouldn't you do whatever it is? What are the implications of applying an idea of prospective use to an area? What are the consequences in terms of costs and benefits? To do this specifically I think would be an enormous improvement to our process. And it seems to me that architects really should be involved in that process. That is, it's an outrage that architects design buildings in flood plains, in areas which are within the smell of volcanoes. Mexico City, thirty million people, is surrounded by volcanoes. Many of them are puffing smoke. This is not a good place to put thirty million people. However, there is something going — we have human stupidity, of course, operating. But there is something wonderfully regenerative. That is, nature accompanies succession.

I went to Korea a couple of months ago to talk about the demilitarized zone. Why? Because these warring people decided to have a neutral belt running right across the whole peninsula two hundred and fifty kilometers long, five kilometers wide. And they put up a 16 foot barbed wire fence on each side, and then left it alone for forty-two years. When they went and looked at it quite recently it's an incredible forest. A large number of animals, and plants, and insects and so on that were thought to be extinct are now not only there, they're abundant! And so suddenly there is regeneration. Then, the eastern seaboard of the United States. I did studies which showed that there are probably more forests on the eastern seaboard of the United States now than there have been since Colonial times. Why? Because all the marginal lands were abandoned for farms early on as people went further and further west. And of course more and more land was abandoned, and continues to be abandoned. And nature solves the problem so absolutely wonderfully. Just walk away, and back comes the forest.

So, can I get a suitable conclusion? Six years ago, to my absolute astonishment I received the National Medal of Art. I've never called myself an artist in my life. I'm a landscape architect. I went to the White House. And there are a lot of wonderful recipients. Beverly Sills, the bosomly operatic lady; Jasper Johns, painter; B.B. King; and others, and me.

FORMATION OF THE TRIASSIC BASIN

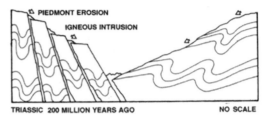

TRIASSIC 200 MILLION YEARS AGO — NO SCALE

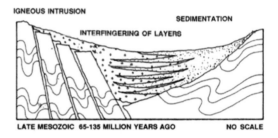

LATE MESOZOIC 65-135 MILLION YEARS AGO — NO SCALE

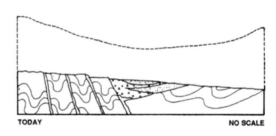

TODAY — NO SCALE

4.07 Geological history as represented in the ecological inventory and analysis coures, University of Pennsylvania, 1993

President Bush gets up and reads a very nice long paragraph — no he doesn't read, recites a long paragraph from my book verbatim, from memory. And then he turns and looks over his spectacles at me, and says "You know, Mr. McHarg, it is my hope that the art of the 21st century will be devoted to restoring the land." Now where did he get that? Who wrote that for him? But that really was quite incredible. I wrote a book you must buy. The publisher said "Ian, we should finish the book by writing a poem to the world's children." And it must have been festering all my life because I sat down and wrote the thing. I only made the original. There are some notes on it but there's only one change in the whole thing. So I'll read it:

"Dearest Children, Do you know that we have inherited a miracle? All matter: the heavens, sun, the Earth itself is made from the ashes of stars. Cycled by volcanoes, and sea, and air, cloud, rain, rivers, rocks, and soils matter permeates us all. Animated including you playing, smiling children now. Exalt in this prodigious, unexpected world. Birdsong and butterflies, puppies and pandas, foals and flowers, dappled trout, the seasons, laughter. You and me joined in this improbable universe. Recoil from the loathsome, mutilated, and scabbed land, foul seas, river, air, squalid slums, wastes, diseased tissues in the living Earth. Repudiate them. Resolve to protect the Earth; it's our home. All creatures are kin. Brethren gifted with light. Aching for fulfilment, doomed to die.

But our breath will fuel flowers. Our tears will join the magic cycle. Our carbon will find other hopes. Our wastes will replenish. In a sense we are immortal as the earth. So you must aim to protect all that's wild and wondrous. To heal mutilations, salve wounds, restore the Earth. Then bequeath a better legacy, a finer future for the Earth and its creatures, for all children now and forever more. Make it a quest for life in God's name."

5.00 NMB Bank Headquarters, Amsterdam: interior space

Buildings as Engines for Environmental Restoration

Bill Browning
Rocky Mountain Institute
Snowmass, Colorado, U.S.A.

5.01 NMB Bank: main lobby volume

So what is a professional environmentalist doing working in real estate development? When Rocky Mountain Institute got into this thing called "green development", we thought of it in terms of habitat protection, buildings to be lighter on the earth, energy efficiency, indoor air quality, and material selection. It is about all these things, but it is also more than that.

We are starting to see something much more interesting emerge. We are seeing it emerge among developers, among designers, even from corporations. We are seeing it come out of environmental groups. And we're seeing it come out of government agencies. Not a lot of it yet, but enough for us to come up and say that green development is a view of real estate development in which you take a real estate development, the act of changing a piece of land, and you use it to generate a financial stream. Yes, it is about making a profit, but you use that financial stream as the engine for undertaking ecological restoration, for financing community development, and even in one case, ethnic dispute resolution. Not what you thought about a real estate developer?

So where is this coming from? In some ways, people are starting to respond to what Aldo Leopold said essentially fifty years ago that to be an ecologist is to

walk through the world and be conscious of the wounds around you. What is happening is people are starting to say that it is time to heal these wounds.

On design juries at architectural schools, I keep hearing all this stuff about layers of meaning for example, "Well, this angle in the building is on the ley line between Sydney and Paris." Great. But if you want a layer of meaning, let's talk about real layers of meaning. What is this building telling me inherently about the culture of place? What is this angle here telling me about the angle of the sun on the solstice? What does this shape here tell me about the nature of the rainfall patterns and the things that are happening on this site? For me, those are real layers of meaning.

Let's talk about buildings where you get the opportunity to address green development issues fundamentally from the outset; the NMB Bank building in Amsterdam. It is a bank that in 1978 had a fairly interesting problem: they were viewed as too stodgy and conservative. Their market share was slipping, and they needed to change the way they were viewed.

So they put together a very interesting way of doing design. It's one that we use frequently, but I wish

5.02 MNB Bank: gardens and courtyards interspersed over the top of a car park and service areas

5.03 NMB Bank: 'Flow-Form' water sculpture integrated with handrail

there was more of it. The building design criteria was only two sentences, from the bank's board of directors. The first sentence was, "It shall be organic, filled with light, air, green, water, art, and happy employees." Number two: "It shall not cost one guilder more per square meter than conventional construction." It is, after all, a bank. Therein lay the challenge.

How did they address this? Well, they put together a team that involved the architect, who had never designed a commercial building before. He had done nineteen thousand housing units, but never a commercial building. Structural engineers, mechanical engineers, electrical engineers, energy experts, bank employees, landscape architects and artists. And the contractors were there as well.

They were instructed they had to work in a team fashion. They had to work around the big table. And if anyone at any point did not understand what was being proposed, it was within their contract that they had to stop the meeting and get a full explanation. Now that sounds like a torturous design process, but it led to a building that is one of our favorites in the world.

The site was chosen by a vote of the bank employees. They chose the site because it was closest to

where most of them lived. There is a half a million square feet sitting on a plinth of three hundred thousand square feet of parking.   The bank sits on the roof of the parking garage. The gardens are entirely watered with rainwater collected in cisterns off the roof of the building, together with a solar collector on top of the towers. The windows have a three-part construction. The center section of the window is for view. There are louvers in the upper section of the windows that bounce daylight into the core of the building. And the bottom section is operable. I show this to most mechanical engineers, and they think I'm nuts, talking about a half a million square foot building with operable windows.

The building is primarily daylit, and somewhat passive solar. The construction technique is all pre-cast concrete. The materials palette is fairly simple. There are no right angles in the building. They got very much into Rudolph Steiner's anthroposophical design, one of the elements of which is that columns tend to be canted various ways and walls are canted in various interesting directions.

At another level there was an interesting collaboration between the energy expert and the artist. Colored pieces of metal on the atrium (one for each of the ten towers) bounce light down to a mirror array on the floor. The walls look green when the green

5.04 NMB Bank: circulation space with interior landscaping

5.05 Lockheed 157: daylighting enhanced by central "litetrium"

metal panels are in the sun. As the sun moves across the sky, at different times of the year and different times of day, it may be yellow, blue, red, orange or pink, depending on the time of day and the time of year.

The building wound up using one-tenth the energy per square foot of their previous building. It cost exactly the market average. But what interests me is more what happened with the bank. Because it so revolutionized their image, they went from being the number four bank of The Netherlands to number two. They have now moved into England and to the U.S. market.

My favorite feature in the whole building springs from it being passively ventilated. What happens in a masonry building with passive ventilation? Well, you get to hear every footstep and every conversation if you don't have the normal hum, clank and rumble of an air handling system. They needed some way to get sound into the building, and they needed to get humidity into the building. So they did that with a cast bronze shape called a flowform. It is basically a stream splashing and gurgling in the hand rail. And it is pretty incredible to see bankers playing with the hand rails.

Now for NMB the most important number of all is what happened with their people. Absenteeism among bank employees is 15% less in this building

than it was in their previous facility. Here is why that is important. Comparative cost of a building on an annual basis is $21 per square foot. Total energy costs are $1.81 per square foot. Meanwhile, office worker salaries are $130 per square foot. If I add in the equipment, benefits and insurance, the cost grows to over $200 a square foot a year.

Let's flip that around. Ten times the rent or a hundred times the energy bill. A 1% gain in productivity is equivalent to eliminating the entire energy bill. What we discovered in a series of case studies is that companies that were driving down the energy use through daylighting, better lighting design, and better thermal comfort significantly raised worker productivity. And they weren't just temporary effects.

Another one of those cases is the $50 million building in Lockheed Martin's engineering production center. Twenty-six hundred employees work there. The building has a very unusual facade. The sloping panes are the view plane, and the vertical panes are light shelves. The floor to ceiling height is fifteen feet. The light shelf enables the light to bounce into the core of the building. In the center of the building is a lightrium. Now this is an integral daylighting device, and it remains a lightrium because at the time it was built, defense contractors were not allowed to have atriums. So this is a lightrium. The building saved half the energy per square foot of a Title 24 standard building, which at the time was the

5.06 Verifone World Distribution Center: existing tilt up concrete warehouse building

5.07 Wal-Mart Eco-Mart: interior showing half of the store

strictest energy code in the country. And the energy measures paid for themselves in four years. However, what Lockheed discovered was the rate of production among their employees increased by about 15%, which allowed them to competitively bid on a contract they would not have otherwise won, the profits from which paid for the entire building.

Another example is a tilt-up concrete warehouse, about as unexciting and unattractive a building type as you could imagine. It was built for Verifone, the folks who make the credit card verification keypads, as their worldwide distribution headquarters in Costa Mesa, California. It was an existing building. It had only three windows in it; because of seismic code, they couldn't add any windows. No punctures in the concrete. All they could do was add daylighting through the roof. Now there are no electric lights on the remanufacturing floor. They work entirely in daylight. They use less than half the energy per square foot of a Title 24 building, the new Title 24.

The entire project was done for $39 per square foot, and in a five-month period. The most interesting number for Verifone is that absenteeism is 47% less among their employees than it was in their previous building. In fact, they have a new problem - they still have a hundred and eighty employees in the old building who are very angry.

Wal-Mart is another of our productivity studies. They pulled us in to help them create their Ecomart. We went through a lot of debate whether or not it would work with Wal-Mart. And we decided that any company that was building one store per working day at a hundred thousand square feet, someone had better talk to them.

One of the fights we had in the building was that our budget got cut for daylighting, and so BSW (the design architects) wound up being able to only daylight half the store. But within two months of operation, because of their Just-In-Time retail, they discovered that the daylit half had significantly higher sales than the conventional half. Wal-Mart is now funding almost more daylighting research than anyone else we have come across.

If we really want to get into the building as pedagogy, this is it: the Boyne River Ecology Center outside Toronto, Canada. It was originally designed as a stand-alone, self-powered building. Unfortunately the maintenance people have incapacitated portions of that. One of the systems that is doing well is the biological waste treatment system, in the center of the building. Raw sewage comes in at one end, and drinking water comes out at the other. School kids that visit here will go to the bathroom so that they can flush and come running and see themselves

5.08 Montana State University, National ReSource Center: innovative designs, materials and construction techniques minimize environmental impact

feed the system.

Now that helped to inspire another building, which is maybe the one that's pushing the furthest. It is the Montana State Green Laboratory Complex in Bozeman, Montana, which hopefully will get under construction in about 1998. Situated in lozenge shapes in front of the building are solar aquatic systems so that the building will treat all of its own waste products.

Using computational fluid dynamics and other energy modelling tools, our current estimate is that — the building being passive solar daylit, passively ventilated and passively cooled — we actually have a problem: we have discovered that in Bozeman there are six days of the year in which we'll need heating. And so we're trying to figure out what to do. We have designed in a series of radiant coils and are going to try to do it that way. So from an energy standpoint, this is a pretty good example.

Bozeman has an extraction economy — much like the rest of Montana. The by-products of that extraction are littering the landscape. Mining waste, agricultural waste, timber waste. And they import most of their building materials. So one of the goals of this project, both from an economic standpoint and from a research standpoint is that as many products

as possible be produced within a three-hundred-mile radius of this building, and be developed in a way that they can then be sold after this building happens. Pliny Fisk helped to develop a fly ash-content concrete slab that's extremely high strength, and lightweight, rastra panels, which are made with a compressed straw aggregate with high insulation value and are very sturdy. Maybe the most interesting product are gluelams from salvaged lumber. That is not all that outrageous until you discover that the adhesive is made from bacteria. It's called Adheron. At the end of the product's life you put it back into an autoclave and introduce an enzymatic key. It unlocks the fibers. You get the pieces of wood back again, and use them in another life span.

If you want to talk about even bigger educational opportunities or institutional buildings, the White House complex since 1993 has been undergoing a renovation called "The Greening of the White House". Part of the building originates from 1792. The Old Executive Office Building was built in 1871. When we arrived there was only one energy meter at the gate. And so a fair amount of the first few months of work was just trying to figure out how and where energy was being used in the building.

One of the things that we discovered, thinking we were so brilliant with Montana and with computation-

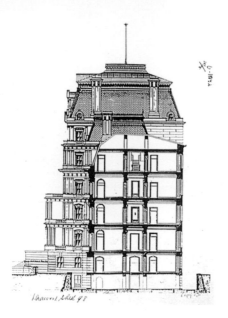

5.09 Old Executive Office Building, Greening of the White House: section showing passive cooling strategy

5.10 Old Executive Office Building: northeast corner built in 1871

al fluid dynamics, is that this building designed in 1871 had one of the most sophisticated passive ventilation systems that we have ever found. The four-foot thick granite walls have air slots running up through them that deliver air into the rooms under the windows; there are transoms over the doors and fourteen-foot-high ceilings, so you allow some of the air to stratify. The rest makes it out into corridors that have glazed domes over them with air vents on top of the domes.

The cupolas over the domes get to 120 degrees Fahrenheit on a summer day. With the vents open, the temperature difference pulls the air column through the building and cools the building. Brilliant design. Unfortunately, the domes were covered with plywood in World War II to black out the building. No one bothered to remove them. In the 1950s stained glass was not modern, so it was painted beige and the holes were covered in. And so the Old Executive Office Building now has seven hundred and eighty-two window air conditioners, one hundred package units and three chillers doing what the building fabric inherently did on its own.

A fair amount of what we're trying to do is to bring the White House back to design intent. How do you do that in a complex that big and address landscaping, indoor air quality issues, recycling streams and-

procurement? Well, a fair amount of that is acheived by pulling together a very large-scale design charette involving over a hundred participants. And that work is now being implemented. The Old Executive Office Building has been reglazed to two panes from one pane with a (low-E) coating and a film that I can tell you exists but would have problems with the Secret Service if I told you what it actually was.

The Executive Mansion will have windows in the solarium on top of the building, and we are looking at electrochromic glass as one option to prevent UV degradation of the historical objects inside. The project has cut the energy bill by over $200,000 a year already, and significantly improved indoor air quality.

One of my favorite measures is on the eighteen acres of grounds. We have found Theodore Roosevelt's original bird list, eighty-five species of birds. Because most of those grounds are forest that people rarely ever hop over the fence and walk through, we have an opportunity to recreate habitat in the fabric of Washington, D.C. And that's what the Park Service is now quietly doing. You can find a lot of this on a CD-ROM from the American Institute of Architects or on a web site called Solstice.

So let's run that kind of thinking out across entire neighborhoods; the Village Homes neighborhood in

5.11 Village Homes, Davis, California: solar heated single family detached homes

Davis, California. It was begun in 1975 by a husband and wife development company, Michael and Judy Corbett. It's based on the plan of Radburn, New Jersey. There are parks, vineyards, orchards, community gardens, community buildings and playgrounds sprinkled throughout the neighborhood fabric. This is an entirely solar subdivision with every building having solar heating.

The streets are substantially narrower than the Davis streets, which had been thirty-two feet wide. They narrowed the streets down to twenty-four feet wide. This number isn't some fanciful number pulled out of the air. This came from taking two fire engines and parking them side by side, unloading them and reloading them as if they were fighting a major fire. That required twelve-foot width per fire engine. And that's how they got the street standard.

By narrowing the street, they generate less impervious surface. The trees are about ten years old and are shading the street and lowering the ambient air temperature over the street by 10-15 degrees Fahrenheit. In a climate that gets to 113 degrees during the summer, that's significant.

The drainage system is the first of its kind in California. It is designed so that water moves through the system in a six-day period. They chose

six days, because after seven they can get a mosquito hatch. About one-third of the water percolates into the ground there, so they use about half the irrigation of a normal subdivision in that area. The city engineer did not think a system like this could work, and in fact he initially rejected it, saying that it would attract vermin. The Corbetts responded that if vermin was the engineering term for wildlife, they hoped they succeeded.

The city required them to put up a performance bond to prove such a drainage system could work. And three years after the completion of Village Homes they had a hundred-year storm event. This was the only system that survived. All the others failed. They got their money back. This drainage system saved them $800 per lot, and that's why they were able to build the vineyards and the community gardens at no additional capital cost.

There is a strip on the western boundary of organic community gardens that actually markets its produce commercially to Chez Panisse, a high-end green restaurant in Berkeley, California. There's a joke among the homeowners that they are happy to be the only subdivision known for the quality of their vegetables. In the pedestrian commons, all the landscaping is edible — fruit and nut-producing trees and shrubs. Literally the way you have breakfast in

5.12 Village Homes, Davis, California: strip of community gardens growing organic produce

5,13 Laguna West, California: one of the first neo-traditional projects designed by architect Peter Calthorpe

the neighborhood is to grab a bowl and go for a walk and find what's ripe.

Now when this was first done, these were middle class homes. They sold for$40-60,000. They ranged from eight hundred to eighteen hundred square feet. The realtors, however, thought this was just too damn weird and refused to show homes there. They said they wouldn't hold value. That was 1976. Where are we at twenty years later? Well, these houses sell for a premium of $11 per square foot. When they come on market, they are on the market less than a third of the market average time. I'd say that's a success.

Laguna West began its life as a thousand-acre site south of Sacramento developed by River West. It was laid out in, as Andreas Duany calls it, the "dead worm" school of land planning, with three thousand homes, 1.25 million square feet of industrial space and three hundred thousand square feet of retail. It had forty-two foot-wide curvilinear streets. Which if they were straight would be great for landing strips, but are pretty poor as a street.

We asked how they got to forty-two foot-wide? And it turns out that Planning and Zoning had one standard; Public Works had another; and Public Safety had a third. They couldn't resolve them, so they

added them together then had some multiplier that they put against it. Thus, forty-two foot-wide streets.

This is a new Californian pattern. There are no front porches on these houses. There aren't even front doors. Only a garage door. You have a front door pulled around to the side for maximum privacy. The developers were then wondering why everyone was demanding security systems for their homes.

Well, that's what Laguna would have been. The developer had political ambitions and was introduced to Peter Calthorpe. Peter rethought Laguna West, and although it still three thousand homes, 1.25 million square feet of industrial space, and three hundred thousand square feet of commercial retail, it is now reorganized into a five-minute walk radius pattern to the village core. The streets are narrowed, and then narrowed even more by putting trees and tree wells along the parking lanes. It unfortunately came onto the market right as the Californian market crashed. So it's gone through a difficult period. But now that the market has come back, the sales are going well.

Because the plan for Laguna West was costed out twice, they know the difference between what it would have cost to do it in the original plan and what it costs now. The addition of the lake, the tree wells,

5.14 Haymount, Virginia: streetscape with a mixture of the 22 different hoousing types

the trees, the decorative lighting and all those other measures, added $1500 to the cost of each lot. The appraisals, however, and I've never considered the appraisal market to capture environmental values very well, came back at f$15000 dollars more per lot.

The builders decided that they would make some of the houses "green". Unfortunately, what they decided they would do is for $5000 add the "Eco Home" package. So for $5000 you get a few better windows, a recycling center in the kitchen sink, you have slightly more efficient appliances, and so on. Those are all good things to do, but they add to the cost of the house. They're essentially plasters tacked on to a standard design.

I want to contrast that with a house built at the same time in Davis, California. It was no stunning architectural statement, and that was intentional. Davis Energy Group took a builder's plans, a house, and modified it from its siblings. What they did was to see how far they could push the energy savings. This was done with Pacific Gas & Electric, who see a ten-year payback horizon.

They had a whole set of modifications, that when analyzed individually, did not meet the payback criteria. They were more than a ten-year payback. But if they bundled them together using DOE-2 modelling,

they discovered that they could eliminate the entire air conditioning system and save $1800 in capital costs in the building. And the building uses 80% less energy than its siblings. And it's more comfortable. You cannot determine the cost of the building by the individual components. It's like an ecosystem. One piece does not tell you all the pieces' value. You have to put all the pieces together. That's how you get a better building.

Haymount, Virginia is a new town for twelve thousand people on the Rappahannock River just south of Washington, D.C. At first, the county thought they would preserve the site by turning it into two, five and ten-acre farms or as Haymount developer John Clark says, martini farms. At that size, it's too damn big to mow, and it's too small to farm, so at best you're going to sit on your back porch, drink martinis and watch the weeds grow.

It is a Duany project. It's neo-traditional. But it's neo-trad with a difference. The houses are picking up on the colonial vernacular. That's partly because you build a contemporary house here and you can't sell it in that market. It's also because we have been learning quite a bit about what the buildings in this region tell us from an energy and materials standpoint. We are going to start a serious exploration of using the lessons as a basis for new architecture.

5.15 Haymount, Virginia: typical block with mixture of housing and commercial building types

Housing types are mixed together in the neighborhoods. Behind a half a million dollar home, on its own lot, a two thousand square foot lot, is an eight hundred square foot cottage that sells for $58,000. One tenth of the units are done this way. This isn't all that outrageous. This is a way we handled affordable housing until about the 1920s. Maybe the place where they're pushing further is the sewage treatment system. The little one in Boyne River was cute. The one in Haymount is treating 1.5 million gallons of sewage a day. Raw sewage comes in at one end; drinking water comes out the other.

The idea of restoration can be very interesting. AT&T were paying $1000 per year per acre in maintaining turf at their corporate campus in Napierville, Illinois. But they weren't doing a very good job of it. They had erosion, and it was pretty awful. So Jim Patchett, a landscape architect in Chicago proposed at $100 an acre, performance-based fee, he would guarantee the creation of a prairie. And the prairie's maintenance consists of burning it once a year. Now for AT&T, that has been the biggest media boon ever. The day that I was visiting the campus, there were wedding parties having their pictures taken in the prairie on a corporate campus.

This brings up another point. From the restored oak savannah, one of the things that we're learning is

that this notion that man has no place in the landscape is utter nonsense. Particularly in the midwest, in these two ecosystems, the tall grass prairie and the oak savannah, these systems only survive with annual burning. That annual burning co-evolved with the native peoples there as the ice sheet pulled back. And it's so pervasive that it's even in their language. The Algonquin word for prairie translates as "the place we burn every year". If you don't burn it every year, the species diversity drops dramatically; in a five-year period you can lose half the species count.

The final project is maybe the most interesting one out there. It is a little hotel in Santa Fe, just off the edge of the historic Governor's Plaza. It's fifty-one rooms and eight suites. It started its life in 1965 as a steel and concrete international-style building right next to the Governor's Plaza — good choice of siting! It was the office building for the State Penitentiary System, and it was a juvenile detention center for Santa Fe. Not exactly an auspicious start for a four-star hotel.

They stripped off the original skin of the building and built a new building in and around it. Almost all the material is locally sourced, with a lot of attention to indoor air quality. The end result is quite beautiful. And as a green building goes, it is a pretty good one.

5.16 Inn of the Anasazi: reused a building that once housed the state penitentiary offices

5.17 Inn of the Anasazi: restaurant interior that features organic foods

Recycling an existing building in an urban fabric, locally sourced materials, good indoor air quality, reasonable energy efficiency, reasonable water efficiency. So you'd say okay, that's a good green building, but why do I care about this one?

Well, this one is about people. This one's about the fabric of Santa Fe. Almost all the furniture here is produced by local artisans. Even the toiletries are produced by a small community north of Santa Fe, using Native American herbs, and are sold through the hotel. The restaurant is a Gourmet magazine top-fifty restaurant. It gets 93% of its food from a network of local organic suppliers, predominantly land grant Spanish families, who if their land goes out of agricultural production get taxed at full development rates and would lose their land. So this gives the family healthy, organic food; gives them income; and it gives them an ability to stay in an exceedingly expensive marketplace.

The restaurant doesn't stop there. They go the next step and close the loop by donating excess food to the homeless shelters. Table scraps are composted and kitchen scraps go to the organic pig farm. Every time we turn around in this operation we find some way that they have proactively woven themselves into the social and environmental fabric of Santa Fe. The staff is made up of the three cultures of Santa Fe. Latino, Native American and Anglo. The staff lead ethnic dispute resolution sessions for the City of Santa Fe. They bring in disputants to the hotel, and the staff lead conflict resolution sessions. This is part of the reason and the operation of the hotel.

Now the guests never find out about this. This is just the way the place is run. What's the end result? Well, there's almost no staff turnover. They are at 83% occupancy, and 50% above their original financial projections. So that's a green project in almost every way I can think. And it really starts to get at Henry David Thoreau's comment: what's the use of a house if I don't have a tolerable planet to put it on?

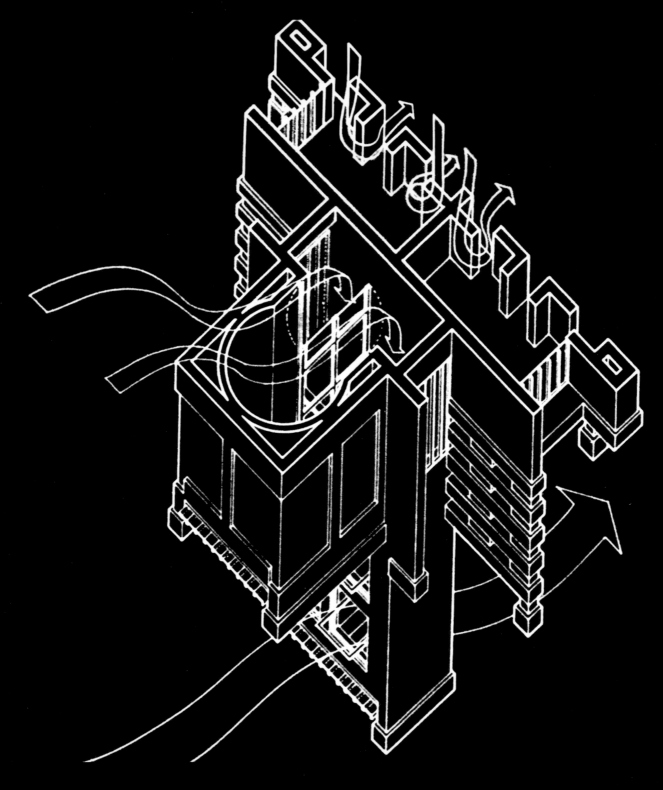

6.00 isometric of passive ventilation and cooling principles. Malta Brewary

The Evolution of a Naturally Conditioned Building Type

Alan Short
Short & Associates,
London, England

6.01 rooftop vents. Malta Brewery

Our practice invents buildings to be as naturally conditioned as possible. More specifically, naturally lit and naturally ventilated. Its larger examples constitute a connected sequence of work in which each successive project benefits from the experience derived from its predecessors. And that's not to say that simulation techniques have obviously evolved at full recognition as far as we can see over the last decade. But we feed off the particular analysis and monitoring of the behavior of our own built work. That is to say, our own physical experience of our own work.

Peter Carolin in Cambridge, England the head of the School of Architecture there, describes our approach as "holistic". While I'm not sure what that means, we think that a naturally conditioned building in which the stuff of its architecture plays a full role in maintaining in a sustainable way, comfort within its enclosures. So it's not just a question of performing some extra remedial work to an existing prototype, though we are regularly asked to. We are by now wholly absorbed in unravelling the consequences of this still not fully understood, all-encompassing role for architectural form.

The first building I will refer to is ironically accommodating and shrouding very high technology. It's a brewery process building within which yeast propagation, fermentation, filtration, sampling, cleansing occur twenty-four hours a day. It meets all the U.S. and European hygene requirements, and it brews beers like Carlsberg on license and a number of other foreign beers. And it makes a living through exports. But it is completely different to the normal type of building for this industry, a rickety tin shed. And it's in Malta in the Mediterranean, which has a California-type climate.

Now our client had decided to look further afield because his original building, which was designed by a London practice in the late 1930s, was very handsome. They had been a little saddened to receive a feasibility study from a brewery consultancy, depicting a rickety tin shed, fully air conditioned. And in Malta, which is a little further south than Tunis in North Africa, August shade temperatures can reach 38-40 degrees centigrade.

However, his lovely 1930s factory was a pretty close copy of the Gillette factory on the Great West Road out of London, including its sawtooth, north light roofs. And in late June in Malta, the sun is not far off the vertical. Of course when we arrived, the north lights were all carefully blacked out. We thought they probably had been after the first week the building was open, to stem the increased instance of sunstroke amongst the employees. As a consequence, the whole factory was artificially lit. This is truly extraordinary, as the sky illuminance might be a hundred thousand lux.

The beer is fermented in open vessels at 7 degrees

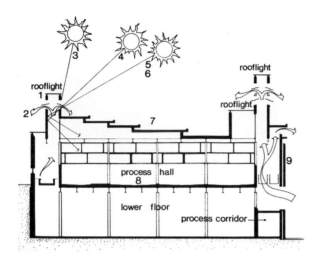

6.02 the cross-section of the building jacket. Malta Brewery

6.03 unsupported masonry elevation. Malta Brewery

centigrade — that's cold — in a huge, multi-story tank building made of four inches of concrete with no insulation, all cooled to 7-8 degrees centigrade. That's a spectacular exercise in which the local town lights dimmed I think regularly as they switched it on. As we've travelled around the world, we see this quite often. We've certainly seen this happening in large buildings in India.

Our building inverts this mid-century strategy. It connects itself directly into the external environment during the night to exploit the potential for naturally induced stack ventilation. And the resulting ventilation heat losses are coupled to a very heavy and massive limestone shell. The building reduces its internal temperature with little or no energy consumption. And each piece of equipment's own refrigeration load inside is reduced accordingly by being placed in a cool environment.

The building is jacketed. It's a volume inside another volume. The space between mediates natural light and air flow. This is not only not a new idea, it's an ancient idea. Certainly not our idea anyway. During the summer day, the building is configured so that the jacket space freely vents while the process chamber is choked to about half an air change an hour. But at night time, or rather as the sun sets, the various timers, temperature and air flow sensors, trigger a small computer program to open the vents connecting the chamber into the vent

stacks. The analysis of forty years of hourly temperature data from the local airport suggested that a pretty high diurnal temperature swing could, on the whole, be relied upon. Not always, but on the whole. And the temperature drops fairly markedly until dawn, regularly enough to hold a night cooling strategy.

And as the outside cools, the building starts to respire. It breathes quite naturally. This is a phenomenon that our Maltese clients wholly understood, but which our UK project managers just would not believe could happen. And we did have a very rough time trying to persuade them. And of course they still do not believe that it actually does happen.

Well for us young architects (we were truly young when we got this project) we were in the bizarre situation of having to use fine-cut ashlar limestone to economize. Limestone's much cheaper than concrete blocks in Malta. This is very odd for me indeed, after my education at Cambridge and at Harvard, and seven years of pursuing notions of thinness and lightness as a partner in Edward Cullinan's office in London.

The constructions on the roof of the building are the size of family houses. They promote the stack effect, and they articulate the building from a distance. We imagined the lights and air towers as "well heads" for raising air rather than water. They also configure a town square

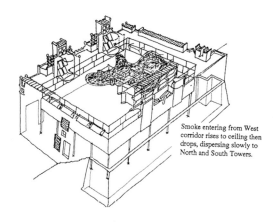

Smoke entering from West
corridor rises to ceiling then
drops, dispersing slowly to
North and South Towers.

6.04 section of elevation showing perimeter ventilation stacks

6.05 Fred, the computer model simulating smoke dispersion.

flying up on the roof, the intention being to resume the big beer dances held by our clients in the late 1940s on the roof of the original building. They haven't had a big dance yet on the top of the house, but we live in hope.

The south elevation of the building receives massive solar attack. It's fifteen meters high, in unsupported masonry. It has no reinforcement in it at all. And its construction is the most elemental imaginable. It has a diaphragm plan form, and within the diaphragm, voids are entrapped which vent the wall during the day to some measurable effect. There's a stack effect taking place inside the construction.

We discovered almost immediately that it was essential to have some form of reliable prediction of the likely performance of the building for the client, for his main board, his funding sources, all the shareholders, the management consultants, the rest of the design team — some of them were very nervous by this stage — and the insurers. We were very fortunate to be able to engage Dr. Nick Baker of Cambridge University who had been developing a finite resistance computer model in which he had incorporated an algorithm for stack ventilation. He called it Fred. We used Fred to simulate a once -in-forty-year heat wave.

So we had a prediction of what would happen in this incredibly unlikely event. And of course I found myself in

Malta in early September waiting to present the project to the main board, in a once-in-forty-year heat wave. A rather elderly man scrutinized this diagram very carefully. The model predicted that the building would start to breathe rather slowly, and then speed up, then take deep breaths, then slow down rather gently towards dawn. Our project managers found this completely baffling and sinister as a proposition.

Early recorded data astonishingly shows very stable temperatures in the process, and an appreciable degree of free cooling. This can and has been quantified in air conditioning plant, capital and more importantly, running costs. In fact, it is precisely this kind of analysis which should enable naturally conditioned buildings to be commissioned more commonly in the medium term. We did have the opportunity to revisit the building with the client and install temperature logging devices which the head brewer, a computer fanatic, downloaded monthly and posted to us in London.

The extended log data from 19 June to 11 July in 1991 shows a gentle fall in internal temperatures, as the night time temperatures are periodically dropping. The internal temperatures vary within a 3 degree centigrade range, whereas externally the temperatures could cheerfully range 20 degrees centigrade in one day. And the buffering effect on dampening heat gain is substantial.

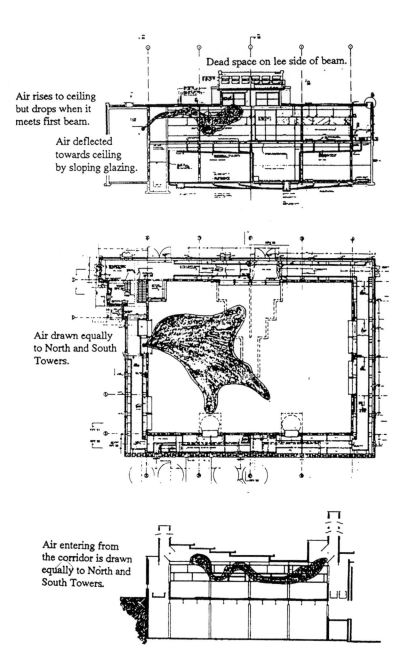

Dead space on lee side of beam.

Air rises to ceiling but drops when it meets first beam.

Air deflected towards ceiling by sloping glazing.

Air drawn equally to North and South Towers.

Air entering from the corridor is drawn equally to North and South Towers.

In still air conditions, cooler air introduced from either side of the building drifts towards all three exit points and some shortcuts around the jacket. But we thought that probably may not be a problem because it is presumably having some kind of beneficial effect. If a wind is blowing over the building, it drives the extracts on the windward side of the building, which is counter-intuitive in a way, but it always happens on the model experiments. And it induces some downdrafting of the stacks at about five meters per second. Now if you're a kind of ventilation physicist, that's the most terrible thing that could ever happen to you. But we don't mind it because the principle, we thought, being a bit more pragmatic, is to flush out the big hole. And we don't really care what direction that happens in.

Then, a rather curious microscale effect showed up: spiralling air flow up the sides of a solar chimney extract. We hope this is a piece of original research, for the observed results fitted, relatively comfortably, the curve of expected air flow rate in still air conditions. Generally speaking, the whole air temperature that we achieved in the June/July period was about 1.5 degrees centigrade below the ambient mean.

That is quite revealing, because it's been found in unventilated, very heavy buildings the internal temperature remains stable at the monthly mean. And in caves the temperature remains at the annual mean. So here the night purging is having some beneficial effect, we found. We'd be anxious to say that, because the client

6.06 the smoke test represented in plan and section

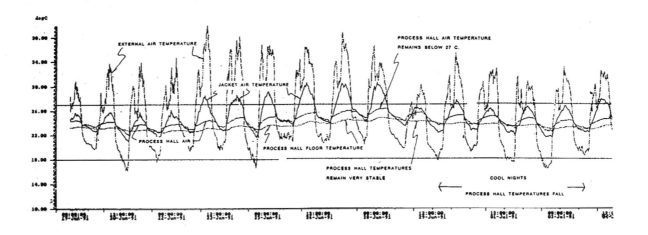

6.07 the recorded internal and external temperature variations:
19 June to 11 July, Malta Brewery

obviously paid a certain amount of money to achieve it.

And here was the most, actually the most terrible and wonderful evening of our lives. This building's supposed to be run by eight people, so all the calculations were showing it running with eight people inside it. Our client arrived in Malta for the opening ceremony and announced that the Prime Minister, the President and the Archbishop were going to open it simultaneously. And they had invited four hundred guests on a July evening. And they told them all they were going to be miraculously cool.

They had opened all the doors up in the building for the day before because they had to move so many chairs in. We contemplated leaving the island immediately. The ceremony started and we sat in the eighth row with a hand-held thermometer. Our eyes were glued to the figures on it. Rather astonishingly the whole ceremony was being televised, so the TV lights were on. It was an enormous, unexpected heat load. We took the precaution of opening the vents up everywhere, and we felt a tremendous breeze develop as the sun was going down outside, and this terrific, appalling heat load was driving the ventilation system at a quite astonishing rate. The temperature rose only 0.5 degrees in two hours. But then as my partner said, the Archbishop was there, so it probably wasn't a reliable scientific experiment.

As the Malta building neared completion, we commenced design work on the new School of Engineering and Manufacture in Leicester for De Montfort University. It was christened by the Queen in late 1993, perhaps a little immodestly, as The Queen's Building. It looks different to the Malta building, which confused some critics, but it is derived through exactly the same method. The intention was to tackle and face this environmental morale problem of the campus and the neighborhood, and to make a building that was as naturally conditioned as possible. It wasn't clear at the outset how far we could reasonably take this strategy, because this laboratory building type has, as far as we could tell, almost always been artificially controlled environmentally in recent times. And the projected heat gains in the various spaces were predicted to demand cooling following conventional practice and institutionalized prescriptions for human comfort. For example, the CIBSE guide, which is the U.K. equivalent of the ASHRAE guide, until recently has been interpreted as a kind of a "bible" on systems performance.

It was only when we started to configure thermally massive laboratory spaces, naturally lit and defended against solar gain, and cross or stack vented with a night purging strategy, that we realized that it might be possible to naturally condition virtually the whole building. Our engineer on this project, Max Fordham, and his colleague Randall Thomas, were encouraging us to be ever more adventurous. Max has located the building by its relative CO_2 production on the spectrum of typical buildings, and it yields some forty-eight kilograms per square meter a year.

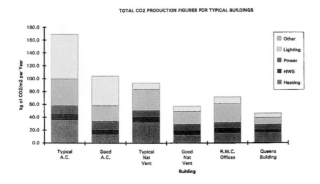

6.08 comparative carbon dioxide levels for different forms of office buildings

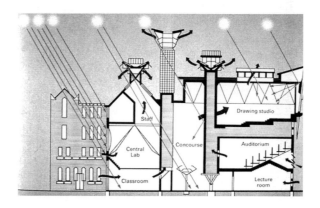

6.09 light and ventilation principles: cross section of the Queens Building, deMontfort University, Leicester

The standard diagram for an engineering school seemed to be that of a deep plan, rectangular building, with three to four floors, with offices and labs arranged around a double-loaded, racetrack corridor plan encircling a large central volume, possibly an open mechanical lab. In fact, we were given drawings of such a building in Sweden as a guide to what was required. And that kind of close-packed diagram definitely describes an artificially controlled building.

The Queen's Building actually is the inverse of this diagram. It assembles wide frontage, narrow section laboratories such as the electronics labs, which can be sideless and cross-ventilated naturally. But then it coils this tight lab section into a deeper plan central building of mechanical labs, classrooms and offices to save site area and internal walking distances. The resulting deeper plan volume is broken open to the sky to admit top light and to exhaust warm, stale air. And an almost freestanding auditorium building sits to the north of the residual concourse. The absence of mechanical air handling plant and hung ceilings allows the top of the building form to be very active and punctured. There's no penthouse plant space which disconnects the occupied part of the building from the sky.

The resulting form and detail of the building are the results of a series of fortuitous coincidences, really, of apparently quite disconnected concerns and enthusiasms. And this opportunity for broader synthesis is what, in our view, makes this kind of design process much more interesting. The architect controls far more of the results amongst an ever-increasing sized orchestra of specialists; physicists, engineers, acousticians, design consultants, clients and legislators. The architect, the profession of the architec, is really more important than ever in this process. I say that because in the U.K. there's a very strong feeling that architects are no longer required.

The essence of the passive strategy is to make a heavyweight, thermally massive building envelope with a high thermal admittance to the very robust swings in external temperature, and to some extent to take up internal gains as well. This is coupled with a judicious ventilation machine tha becomes more judicious as it's tuned in use, which is a very important part of the recipe. This intent coincides with our enthusiasm, which was developed in Malta, for low-gain masonry. It's expressed in the way in which one might manipulate it to develop openings, large voids, large free-standing panels, all unframed.   It's very important in terms of the physics not to obscure too much of this mass internally, inviting its expression. And here we've used pressed calcium silicate brickwork internally in a Flemish bond. We have developed a certain expertise in bonding brickwork, which is a fascinating science, and in expressing its actual construction through polychromatic differentiation of the necessary layers that make the bond structurally cohesive.

6.10 vents in the brick elevation: Queens Building, Leicester

6.11 elevation to Mill Lane, Leicester.

Now some spaces require reconnecting to the outside air. The air change rate is stimulated by a natural thermo-siphonic air movement which is induced by the provision of stacks. And they're formed as four-foot square, bonded masonry chimneys. The upper part's buttressed by additional brickwork. The masses are lifted off the floor by steel props, treated in thin film intumescent paint. I think this may have been one of the first buildings to use this product to any scale — it lets you expose steelwork structurally with a good finish.

The whole notion of lifting a building up on iron was invented by Viollet-le-Duc, and revived here to offset an unhealthy characteristic of masonry buildings, the very occluded ground floor plans that they naturally develop. The development of the new smooth-coated intumescents make this quite legal in terms of the fire codes. And the intermediate floor structure is a double T precast plank sitting on pad stands. It's really multi-story car park construction.

The emphasis on puncturing levels to bring natural light to the ground floor and allow warmed air to rise and escape resulted in the excessive cutting away of floor structures, to the huge amusement of our engineers, and may seem to be just beyond their natural integrity. In each case, sunlight is still properly employed. The intention is to deinstitutionalize the building, and this is expressed partly through the high degree of indivisibility between spaces. That is achieved by the use of very carefully distributed areas of one hour fire-resistant glaz-

ing, which is blindingly expensive.

The context of The Queen's Building in Leicester is prototypical in some respects. It's a fragmented, quarter-rebuilt city center with a depressed economy and extensive demolition sites dating from the 1960s. Our hypothesis is that the building could attempt to strike a rhythm with its immediate natural environment, and could also attempt to opportunistically exploit this inherently more flexible form; more flexible than a racetrack plan and a cubic volume. To plug a hole in the urban landscape — that is still a radical notion, it seemed to us.

Of course the first question is, is the hole at all worth filling with any recollection of what was there before? Well, the former planning officer in Leicester thought absolutely not. This was his vision of Leicester: wholesale demolition. Subsequently, certainly when I was at Harvard, they were pursuing Robert Venturi's tendency to review and re-review pre-existing buildings and settlement patterns proactively.

We were very intrigued by the residual forms of the streets in Leicester which had survived the superimposition of a system building grid in the early 1960s. For example, Mill Lane, which is the street our building sits on, shows up in maps from the 1740s, and by 1888, it had developed into a busy street. There was a whole community here. It was widened to take public buildings the corners of the post office and various public houses. Exactly a hundred years later, the block plan had experi-

6.12 the end elevation of the laboratory wing. Queens Building, Leicester.

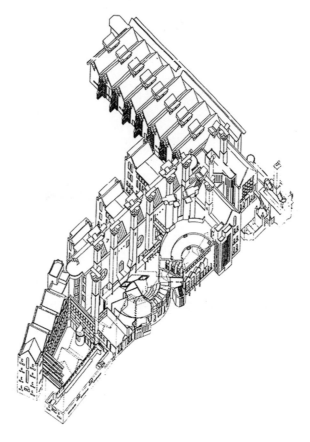

6.13 the composition of the major parts of the project, represented in three dimensions

enced a massive destruction as a result of the demolitions.

The building form is gone, but the ground plan preserved its vestigial street patterns. This is a phenomenon that I recall seeing in red-lined areas in St. Louis, where I was sent to survey by my American bosses in New York. We took a particular attitude to the authenticity of the remains here in Leicester, and we pursued the exhumation. Teaching in Leicester, I was introduced to the latest market area of Nottingham which is an industrial area, in which very large buildings occupy the interiors of blocks but reinforce the street pattern. The building type was also ingeniously adapted to supply high levels of natural light into the upper floors, which is called "making lace". It's an incredibly delicate exercise for which an engineer would provide two or three thousand lux artificially now. And I say that this is an ingenious exercise because the Florentine and Alpine prototypes for many of these buildings did exactly the reverse. Anyway, this is a clue to the nature of Leicester before so much of it was demolished.

The Queen's Building offers a variety of environmental strategies. The constituent parts are highly differentiated in their configurations and so it is really a collection of buildings. The most ambitious exercise is the eliminationof mechanical air handling and cooling in the two principal amphitheaters. The auditorium form represents the opportunistic and simultaneous play of completely different sets of intentions: theatrical ideas, acoustic,

educational, thermal, air movement notions, all promoted by different interest groups.

Firstly, there's our client's teaching ambition of bringing the audience as close to the speaker as possible using a Greek amphitheater pattern. This is a full hundred and thirty-five-degree fan theater with a very steep rake, to seat a hundred and sixty people in the auditorium. This necessitated a theater arrangement where you put everyone in very long rows, but you give them a bit more room to squeeze past each other, so you eliminate the aisles. These are straight theatrical ideas.

Then there is the goal to reduce or to remove a dependence on mechanical air handling and cooling for a host of generally acknowledged, compelling environmental reasons. This brings into play an imperative to make the enclosure as massive and as heavy as possible for thermal reasons, to make controllable air inlets and exits,

6.14 the interior of the main concourse, the auditorium to the right and ventilation chimneys to the left.

6.15 the interior of the naturally ventilated auditorium

routes and stacks, and to make chambers in the way of them, filled with acoustic veins to absorb external noise en route.

Next, we sought to exploit the mass of the masonry stacks to support the roof. We always do that, because in Britain there's a profession you don't have in the U.S. called the "quantity surveyor" who's in charge of the cost control of the project. So we always make our natural ventilation devices — particularly since our experience with the English project managers in Malta — so essential to the structure of the building they can't be sliced out just before they're being built. So they're always holding a lot of the building up.

The controls for air flow in the auditoria function in a very similar way to those in the rest of the building. There are, however, many more sensors in the auditorium. This allows a greater degree of control over the space. The basic requirement is for a liberal supply of fresh air, here ten liters a second per person. For enough air to provide the required cooling, the dampers on the stacks will open to cool the room as required. At times, of course, it is possible to cool the building down below its heating set point in the summer. And there's an attempt in the software to prevent the building from being reheated the following morning.

The allowable temperatures were established physically

— this is most interesting. The vice chancellor gives a good talk about how he commissioned this building. If you throw away the ASHRAE guide or the CIBSE guide where does everybody stand? That is, what is a reasonable temperature — how hot or cold should one be allowed to get? It was decided that 27 degrees centigrade for limited periods, very limited periods, constituted the upper boundary of the comfort zone.

Well, the vice chancellor established the allowable interior temperature physically by taking the working party client group of thirty-two people and holding meetings in a series of different rooms in the university during the summer with a series of temperature recording devices in the room. We found that we'd all been sitting in rooms at 32 degrees centigrade quite happily, arguing about the building.

The building is being continuously monitored, and very encouraging heat load tests were conducted, again by accident, in June 1994. In Leicester, this was a one- in-forty-year fantastic heat wave. We found it was very difficult to raise the internal temperatures beyond 23.5 degrees centigrade. The outside temperatures were getting towards 31 degrees centigrade. And the good people of Leicester were really panicking that afternoon because of the appalling heat.

Subsequent analysis of the electricity and gas

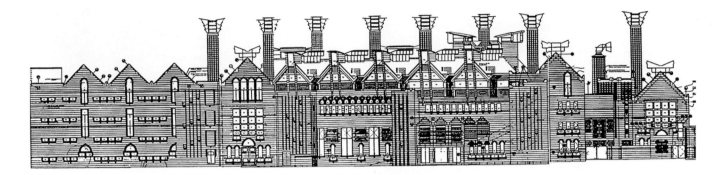

6.16 architects drawing of the elevation to Mill Lane

consumption was also quite encouraging. It's a one hundred and ten thousand square foot building. It consumes some one and a quarter million kilowatt hours of gas a year, and four hundred and thirty-odd thousand kilowatt hours of electrical energy. But that includes all the loose equipment loads and all the computers and equipment inside the building. Unfortunately, we are unable to disaggregate an actual building load.

In the "mechatronics:" laboratory, the electrical, electronics and mechanical engineers on the whole don't speak to each other. So the building is arranged so that they can meet in a common laboratory and invent electro-mechanical mechatronics type things, which is what they're supposed to be doing. It's completely naturally lit and naturally ventilated, and seems to be reasonably successful. Again, it's fully glazed, but we tend not to go off to Pilkington's in Britain, which show you how to make spectacular, vast areas of glass all welded together. We've just stacked up something like twenty-four domestic-sized windows in a kind of sandstone screen to keep them shaded, a more modest approach. The sad thing is that the engineering design used to happen in little leaking, portable buildings on the site before the building was built. Designing and inventing engineering things was associated with getting wet and being cold and no prestige. So we put the design studios in the best part of the building, up in the attics. They're actually open to the concourse space, which is a slightly dangerous academic thing to do. But everyone's got used to keeping quiet in the concourse, which is rather nice.

Our mechanical laboratory has a noise issue, and again we've used a diaphragm construction. The buttresses are bracing a mechanical crane with a travelling crane inside. But we use the diaphragm, the voids within the buttresses, to kill sound as air gets in and out of the building. The electronics laboratories have spectacular heat output theoretically, like eighty-four watts per meter. They would certainly be air-conditioned in Europe, but in Leicester they are very narrow rooms, and cross-ventilated. Sixty percent of the elevation can be opened up. But it never has been; the occupants haven't had to resort to the maximum capacity of the building at all. This is very interesting, because in some sense it means that the scale of the environmental problem isn't as awful as everyone imagined it to be.

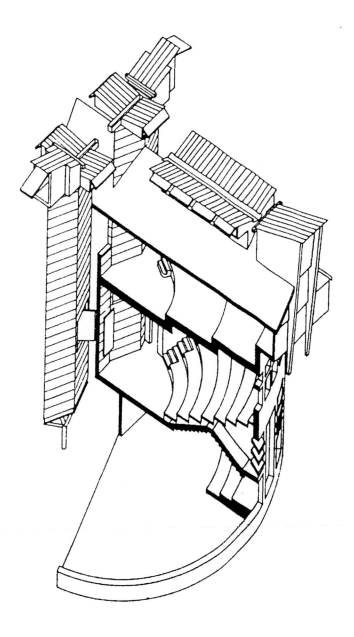

6.17 cut-away section of the auditorium with drawing studios over, and ventilation chimneys

William McDonough
University of Virginia

7.00 Warsaw Beauty, a project for a skyscraper in Poland,
with 10 square miles of trees to offset the energy and climatic
consequences

Declaration of Interdependence

William McDonough
University of Virginia
Charlottesville, Virginia, U.S.A

7.01 Tri Art project: an explorartion in the fusion of art and architecture by Willam McDonough and Partners

It's very clear that Thomas Jefferson saw himself as a designer. You realize that he saw himself as a designer clearly when you look at his tombstone, which he designed. On it he remarked three things, and three things only. It says "Thomas Jefferson, author of the Declaration of American Independence, author of the Statute of Religious Freedom for the State of Virginia" which became the Bill of Rights, and "Father of the University of Virginia". Three things he considered his legacies. He didn't record any of his activities. He didn't say "President of the United States, Minister to France". He simply left messages about his legacies.

If we look at the Declaration of Independence as a retroactive design assignment we could say that it would be a system that allows for the pursuit of life, liberty, and happiness free from remote tyranny. Let's think about this idea of remote tyranny. Mr. Jefferson clearly understood this concept of remote tyranny; in his day it would have been represented by George III, by a person. Today, the remote tyranny is intergenerational. Jefferson clearly understood this idea of intergeneration. In 1789 he wrote a letter to James Madison in which he said "The earth belongs to the living. No man may by natural right oblige the lands he owns or occupies to debts greater than those that may be paid during his own lifetime, because if he could then the world would belong to the dead, and not to the living." The world would belong to the dead. The Chief of the Onondaga People was

recently at the University of Virginia. He belongs to the sixth nation in the direct line of the great Iroqouis confederacy which declares that all chiefs should make decisions on behalf of their seventh generation. As we were walking down the lawn it occurred to me that we are Thomas Jefferson's seventh generation. You are it. He wrote the Declaration of Independence for you. It's our turn to write 'Declarations of Interdependence' for our seventh generation. In order to do this we have to come up with some design principles.

In the Declaration of Independence, Jefferson uses the concept of "natural rights" all the time. I think we can flip the Declaration of Independence to the Declaration of Interdependence, we can flip the concept of natural rights and look at the rights of nature. So what are the rights? And what is the history of rights? In our tradition, the history of rights can be tracked to Magna Carta 1215, the rights of white noble males, to the Declaration of Independence, the rights of white land-owning males (which comprised only 6% of the population), to the Emancipation Proclamation, to Native Americans, who in 1923 were given the right to vote, to the Civil Rights Acts of the 1960s, and to 1973, when for the first time in history humans have given something other than humans the right to even exist: the Endangered Species Act. And now we're talking about endangered ecosystem acts. We can see that the evolution of rights is leading us to the understanding that

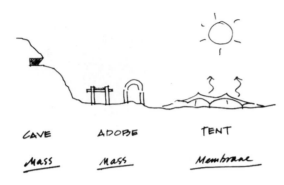

7.02 forms that understand the principles embodied in mass and membrane. sketch by Willam McDonough

7.03 Tri Art project: experimenting with mass, membrane, transparency

nature itself should have rights.

We need to look at what nature is. Only in understanding that nature is where we are and where we live do we understand that we ourselves have rights. Only by understanding that, understanding our home, can we respect ourselves. How do we find kinship with nature? How do we find ourselves at our rightful place in nature? In the Native American tradition, how do we find our kinship with nature? Well what is nature? Ralph Waldo Emerson in 1838 wrote an essay on nature entitled "Nature" for Harvard. And in it he explored the question if human beings are natural, are therefore all things produced by human beings natural? And his conclusion was that nature is all those things that are immutable — the things too big for humans to affect — the oceans, the mountains, and the leaves. Well I think Thoreau probably knew a little better. And I think we now understand that we could and can affect the oceans; and we can affect the mountains; and we can affect the leaves. There is this concept of "away". That you could throw something away. Well away has gone away. The Californians are going to Washington, the Washingtonians are going to Alaska, the Eskimos are nervous. There is no "away". And we've now come to understand that in our time. If there is no away, and nature is mutable, perhaps we do have dominion over nature. Perhaps we do have to have implicit stewardship, and that perhaps implies kinship. And if kinship is our intention, then we have to

begin to understand our design because design is the first signal of our intention.

So what is design? In 1832 Emerson went to Europe when his wife died. And he went over in a sailboat, and he returned in a steamship. Let's abstract this for effect. He went over in a solar powered recyclable craft operated by a craftsperson practicing ancient arts in the open air. And returned in a steel rustbucket putting oil on the water, smoke into the sky, operated by people working in the darkness shovelling fossil fuels into the mouth of a boiler. We are in a steamship right now. We're still designing steamships. We haven't figured out what the next ship looks like. So what is design? Well that ship is a design. Peter Senge at MIT in the Organizational Learning Center has a leadership lab. And the first question he asks of the leaders coming in is: who is the leader on a ship crossing the ocean? And the answers he gets, as you can imagine, are captain, navigator, helmsman, so on. And he says no, it's the designer of the ship. Because you can be the best captain in the world, the best navigator; but if the ship is not seaworthy you are going down. And so the designer of the ship is the leader. And therefore leaders must become designers, designers must become leaders. We are the designers; we are the leaders. But in order to do this work we're going to need some principles. Because we are still in the dark.

7.04 Tri Art project: south elevation represents agriculture, east and west are water, and the north elevation is the earth tipped up.

7.05 solar heated, solar illuminated factory for Herman Miller by William McDonough and Partners.

I would like to give you a design assignment. I want you to think about it as I give it to you. Is this an ethical assignment I am giving you? I would like you to design a production system for this country that produces billions of pounds of highly hazardous toxic material, and puts it into your soil, your air, and your water every year. I would like you to design a system that measures prosperity by how much of your natural capital you can cut down, dig up, burn, bury, otherwise deplete, and destroy. I would like you to design a system that measures progress by the number of smokestacks, and if you're especially proud of them you could put your name on them. I would like you to design a system that measures productivity by how few people are working. While you're at it make it require so many thousands of complex regulations because actually you have to give people license to kill. The question is how long will they have before it's terminal? Do you want to be hung or do you want to be shot? And just on the side, produce a few things that are so highly toxic and volatile that they will require thousands of generations to maintain constant vigilance while living in terror. Can you do that for me? That is the retroactive design assignment. That is the retroactive design assignment of the first Industrial Revolution; and we are in the middle of it. The only principle of the Industrial Revolution, I have discerned, is that if brute force isn't working you're not using enough of it. We are still promulgating it. So we need some new design assignments, and we had better get going.

The New York Regional Plan Association has just published its regional plan. And the figures that are included in it are quite astonishing. In 1940, the impervious surface of the New York City region — roads, parking lots — was 18%. In 1996, it was 42%, and the projection for 2015 is 82% impervious surface. What is the temperature? What does the water look like? Where are the songbirds? And where do all the children play? If that is the tragedy that we now project then we could say that once you project the tragedy, you have the tragedy. You are vested in that tragedy. And that means that that must be your intention because you're allowing it to occur. And if you're allowing it to occur then you have adopted a strategy of tragedy. And the only way to cure a strategy of tragedy is to adopt a strategy of change immediately. So I would like to posit a strategy of change with some new design principles. And these principles are simple. And here's the design assignment for the next industrial revolution: could you design a system that doesn't release any hazardous material into your soil, or your air, and your water? That measures prosperity by how much of your natural capital you can accrue and invest infinitely? That measures productivity by how many people are working? That measures progress by buildings that have no pipes? That doesn't require thousands of complex regulations because we're not trying to kill each other? And we will not produce anything that requires future generations to maintain vigilance or live in terror? That sounds like a more

7.06 the daylit street to the Herman Miller factory in Michigan

7.07 low energy building for the Gap corporate campus, California by William McDonough and Partners

reasonable design assignment.

The principles that we use in our work are three. Waste equals food. Use current solar income. Nature does not mine the past, it does not mortgage the future.

If waste equals food then there's no such thing as waste. If there's no such thing as waste, then what we're trying to do here is not minimize waste — we're trying to eliminate the entire concept of waste. This is not ecoefficiency. Ecoefficiency means I wake up in the morning, and I feel really bad. The world is terrible. And I'm going to spend my entire day trying to feel better by being less bad. Is this a noble day? So I'm going to spend my whole day trying to feel better by being less bad, and my goal is zero. I don't have to reimagine the world in this scenario. I just live with it the way it is, and I just try and be less bad. That to me is a really boring prospect. What we're looking for is what does 100% sustainable look like? So I wake up in the morning and I say "Well I'm only 20% sustainable today, but tomorrow I'm hoping to be 21." Now I have to imagine what 100 looks like. And that's a creative agenda. And that's what we need. We require massive creativity, massive openness, massive change.

The principle of waste equals food means that we have to look at the planet as a series of metabo-lisms. There are fundamentally two metabolisms. One is organic metabolism of which we're physically a part; and the other is what I call the technical metabolism, the industrial metabolism. I work with a chemist in Germany, and we've articulated two types of products. Products of consumption that you truly consume, go back to the organic cycles. They go back to soil safely. No mutagens, no carcinogens, no heavy metals, no persistent toxins, no bioaccumu-lative substances, and no endocrine disrupters. Other materials, products of service, go back to the industrial cycles. What you really want is the service of the thing, not necessarily the ownership. If I took a television set, and I said "I know this amazing thing, provides astonishing service. But before I tell you what it does let me tell you what it is. You tell me if you want this in your house. It is 4360 chemi-cals, 18 grams of highly toxic mercury, it has an explosive glass tube, and we think you ought to put it at eye level with your children, and encourage them to play with it. Do you want this in your house?" Why are we selling people hazardous waste? What you want to do is watch TV, not own 4000 chemicals. We need a new design. This should be seen as a "product of service". And we have trademarked this term now because we're applying it to design proto-cols. We developed the concept because it basically says take a product like this and design it. If waste equals food, then this is part of the industrial metabo-lism. This is a nutrient, a technical nutrient of what industry? The electronics industry. So let these

7.08 external wall model for Gap corporate campus, combining with nightime cooling through the thermal mass the floor slabs

7.09 the perforated nature of the Gap building - capable also of being converted to housing in the future.

companies that design these products take them back. So when you finish with it you say "Thank you so much for the service. I enjoyed watching television. I'd like a new television please." And this becomes something designed to go back to technical cycles forever, and not be released.

We are doing that with carpets. We are working with the Interface Corporation, and we have developed a products service protocol for them. Paul Hawkin wrote about our work in his book "Ecology of Commerce". It was picked up by a man named John Picard, who talked to the chairman of Interface. The chairman came back to us and we are designing the products based on our concepts. We're redesigning his carpets so that they'll go back to being carpets forever. He will lease the services of the carpet. It will be flooring services. Comfort, acoustics, visual pleasure, and so on. He won't be selling carpets. Because our point to him was that since 1973 when he started his carpet company he's made four billion pounds of carpet. Where is it? Cradle to grave typology. What we want is what I've coined as a cradle to cradle life cycle assessment. If he had used our protocol, which we're just getting patents on right now, he would still own four billion pounds of carpet of technical nutrient for his industry. The street value as used goods is about 1.4 billion dollars. His corporation would still have an asset on the bottom line of 1.4 billion dollars. Think about it. If our countries and companies expect to be wealthy in the future they

should accrue natural capital forever rather than deplete it. This chairman has committed not to take one drop of petroleum in the future if he can; and we're working with him on that process. So the only kind of products we should have are consumables that go back to soil; products of service that go into technical cycles forever, and never see landfills.

Sustainability is really a shibboleth. It's just a code word for maintenance. It's not going to help us. Sustainability is the edge, halfway between destruction and restoration. Sustainability is not that interesting. Just maintain what we've got now. We actually have to go into what we call a restorative agenda. Because we've been in a destructive agenda for so long we actually have to start restoring. So we're looking at how to make buildings that are like trees, that are fecund. They make more energy than they need to operate so they are net energy exporter buildings. We're also looking at buildings that treat water like healthy soil: they absorb it quickly, and release it slowly in a pure form rather than vice versa. We're talking about designing sites without pipes. We're talking about whole landscape protocols where we don't use pipes at all. So the water is celebrated as a biological matrix rather than as chemistry suffering from physics. We're looking at diversity not just as people but of systems. We're saying "All sustainability is local." Materials will have to come from where you are. The question will have

7.10 the Oberlin Building by William McDonough and Partners: net energy exporter using a photovoltaic roof.

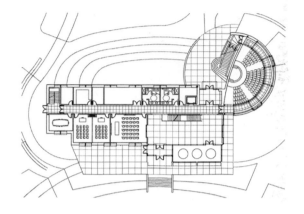

7.11 plan of Oberlin Building: the clerestory lit public space leads to the auditorium via a 'living machine' and classrooms.

to first be "Where are you?"

Ecoefficiency really has me worried. Everybody keeps saying "nature is efficient". Nature is not efficient. You don't walk down the Mall in Washington in the spring, look at the cherry trees and go "Boy, these trees are inefficient". How could they possibly need all those blossoms? They're just trying to get one cherry to recreate here." How about human sperm? 500,000 human sperm just so one can get lucky. Nature is fecund. Nature loves abundance. It's not based on limits, it's based on abundance. It's based on this sort of joyous outpouring. And the thing is that all that outpouring is safe. It returns to the soil. So efficiency is really not what we're after here. We're looking for something I think a little richer than that.

So let's take a quick look at what happens when you use this for design. We were asked to design a fabric by Steel Case Corporation. We said "Well that's nice. You know, we'd love to do that. We'd also need to design not just what it looks like but what it is." And they said "Well we figured you'd say something like that so we've come up with it. It's cotton mixed with PET. Natural cotton, PET recycled. It's natural, recycled, got all the green words. Isn't that great? It's strong, it's cheap." We said "Well wait a minute. Is that an organic nutrient? Does that go back to soil safely? Not with the PET. Does that go back to an industrial cycle safely? Not with cotton."

Oh, that's interesting. A product that should not be made. How often have you heard that? A product that should not be made. Now let's look at our six criteria. Cotton is responsible for over 20% of the world's use of pesticides. It causes hydrological disasters. And it has never been associated with social fairness. PET is a petrochemical product that includes antioxidants, UV stabilizers, plasticizers, and antimony residues from catalytic reactions. And it does not belong anywhere near human skin. Why would I want to use either of these materials in this fabric under current production technique? So we developed our own product based on using wool from happy sheep in New Zealand, and ramie, an organically grown nettle in the Philippines. Ramie is a wick, it's very strong. Stronger than steel in tensile strength. It holds the fabric together and wicks away moisture. And the wool absorbs moisture. It keeps you cool in the summer, warm in the winter. We interviewed people in wheelchairs to determine what we needed for sitting. And it turned out that moisture is their biggest problem. So we designed a fabric that absorbs moisture and that wicks it away.

Well that was great. When I arrived at the mill when we started this project, the owner of the mill in Switzerland, the president, had just had the trimming of his bolts of cloth declared hazardous waste by the Swiss government. Isn't that interesting? The trimming is declared hazardous waste. You can't bury or burn it in Switzerland, but you can sell what's in the

7.12 Oberlin Building model of the northern elevation.

7.13 the green office: project for the Environmental Defense Fund, New York by William McDonough and Partners.

middle. You don't need to be Einstein to work out that you're selling hazardous waste. So I said "What if you could make your trimming into compost?" So we worked on this fabric. We did an organic nutrient fabric. And we got the wool, and we got the ramie, and we got the fabric going. And then we needed to do the colors, the dyes, the finishes, the fire retardants, and so on.

We went to sixty chemical companies and said "In the future, design filters will be in our heads rather than on ends of pipes. We won't have filters in smokestacks, and we won't have filters on pipes. Here's the design filter — no mutagens, no carcinogens, no heavy metals, no persistent toxins, no bioaccumulatives, no endocrine disrupters. Who wants to work with us?" Sixty companies immediately shut the door. It was amazing how quickly they communicated. And so we went to the chairman of Ciba Geigy in Basle, and we said "We need to do this." He said "You're right." He let us in, we looked at 8000 chemicals in the textile industry. And with that filter we had eliminated 7962. We were left with 38 chemicals. We did the entire fabric line with 38 chemicals. The most important part of the story was when the Swiss inspectors came to the mill to inspect the effluence after our product was run. They thought their equipment was broken. They couldn't find anything. They went and tested the inflow on Swiss drinking water. Sure, the equipment was fine. Turned out that the fabrics were filtering the water. The water coming out was cleaner than the water going in. When you reach the point where your effluent of a factory is cleaner than the influent which is Swiss drinking water, guess what happens, you can cap the pipe. You'd rather use your effluent than influent. There is no pipe coming out of the factory. There is no regulation because there's nothing to regulate because we are not trying to kill each other. As you watch ecoefficiency happen, you watch people do toxic reductions. We see that their cadmium release is lower, and lower, and lower, and the thing that makes me nervous is that means often that the cadmium is now being stored in their product. And their product is becoming a worse and worse emission. And they put it in trucks, and they sell it. I call this the flag of the next industrial revolution.

In Chattanooga, we've created something called zero emissions zoning. When people said "How can you do zero emissions zoning?" all we had to do was point to our factory in Switzerland, and then borrow from Amory Lovins and say "It exists, therefore it is possible." The first company to sign up for the protocol was Dupont. Dupont is declared for zero emissions. We've had zero accidents, we've had zero defects, we've had just-in-time delivery which is zero inventory. Now it's time for zero emissions. The city is undergoing a phenomenal transformation of its downtown, but as Dave Crockett says "If we just deal with the downtown and we don't tackle sprawl, it's

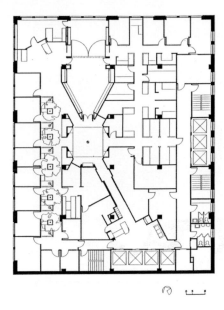

7.14 offices as little buildings along a street: plan for Environmental Defense Fund, New York.

7.15 the interior street: Environmental Defense Fund, New York

like getting a facial while you have your wrists slit." You're going to look fabulous at the funeral. At the University of Virginia we are building an addition to the architecture school that will be a net energy exporter as well. We are using Stephen Holl from New York, and Michael Van Valkenberg, a landscape architect from Harvard, as our design team; they have to work together. These are people who are celebrated for their art. And so the idea that we would have people perceived in the architectural professions as artists working with these issues is very exciting.

At the University of Virginia we are also setting up an Institute for Sustainable Design to bring together all the disciplines within the University. The Law School, the Engineering School, the Business School and the Medical School, to work on collaborative projects together as designers. We're going to take on glass fiber as a carcinogen. We're going to be taking on endocrine disrupters in the built environment. We'll be taking on photovoltaics, flywheels, designing landscapes without pipes and transportation. In the School of Architecture alone we have 42 proposals that relate to sustainable interdisciplinary work within the Architecture faculty. It's an initiative of the entire University, it was announced by the president, it's being funded by the University, and will involve everyone on the grounds.

So the question is again this one of how do we love

all the children? What is our legacy? I'll give you one example of what happens when you start to think about loving all the children from Curitiba. I was there this summer meeting with Jaime Lerner. Jaime Lerner is an architect who was the mayor of Curitiba, Brazil. And when the city of Curitiba decided it was time to build a library, instead of doing as they did in San Francisco by building a $128 million dollar mausoleum for books, they said "How do we build a library, and love all the children?" Not just some of the children, all of the children. Well that doesn't mean you put all your money in the civic center, and whoever can afford the time and the money to get there gets there even if they have the best public transit in the world.

They decided what they would do is take their budget, and divide it up, and they built libraries that look like little houses with lighthouses on the front of them. They're to be located within 12 minutes walking distance from every single child in the city. And a forester, or a police person, or a teacher, or a parent sits inside this lighthouse and makes sure the kids are safe coming to the library. And when they get there they have all the books they need for school. And if they want to buy textbooks and they can't afford them, they can trade garbage for books. Every child has access to books. The books are printed on recycled paper in the city's own presses. Also every child will have access to the World Wide Web. How do you design a library, and love all of

7.16 daylit offices for the renovated interior of the Heinz Family: using sustainable forestry techniques in the various woods that were used in the project, that preserve local diversity.

7.17 lobby space of the interior for the Heinz Family, by William McDonough and Partners

the children? As Jaime says "A train can only go as fast as its slowest car."

So this is our question. How can we do that while we restore songbird habitat? How do we exercise human artifice as artifact worthy of leaving to future generations? How do we honor that sacred thing in ourselves that lets us do things like that? That allows us to think about things that rise up from the earth, and that can return to it safely forever. How do we not produce tragedies for our future generations? And how are we going to allow them to pursue life, liberty and happiness, free from remote tyranny when the remote tyranny is us?

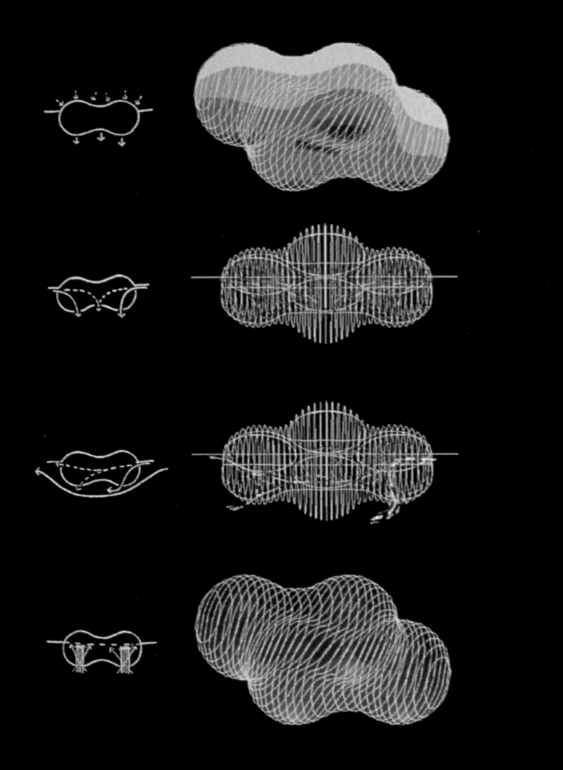

8.00 form finding from the natural forces of gravity

The Need and Drive for Sustainable Architecture and Urban Design

Christopher McCarthy and Guy Battle
Battle/McCarthy Engineers
London, England

8.01 the naturally ventilated Ionica Building, Cambridge, UK.

Christopher McCarthy:
There are many different definitions of sustainability. To engineers, our definition of working is to maximize uses of materials, skills, and energy for the benefit of mankind. That's always been our goal. Architects and society define the benefits. Architects are redefining what "benefit to mankind" means, but as engineers we are progressing in the direction of improving the efficiency of their work. We believe engineers can only be as good as the architects they work with, and vice versa. That's one of the issues we work at constantly: the working relationship between architects and engineers. If the relationship is improved we end up with more efficient design. There's little doubt about that.

So where does the debate begin? There's a lot of historical precedents. But what is really missing often in discussion between the engineer and the architect is the fundamental issues associated with building physics. It is common sense: hot air rises, gravity pulls us towards the ground, wind pushes buildings over. These are the three forces that we, as engineers, work with. And, as engineers working with architects, I feel that the boundaries between our disciplines are fading.

Battle McCarthy engineers the built environment with architects. The "built environmen'" ranges from master planning, developing new towns of 15,000 people outside Cambridge; to the largest sustainable regen-

eration in Europe, the development of the peninsula of Greenwich in Central London; and to individual buildings such as the Ionica Building, a building that is not dependent on mechanical ventilation, and not dependent on artificial lighting. But you have a choice. We're not saying the sole goal is to make a daylit building, and the sole goal is to make a naturally ventilated building. What is important is that we understand the brief we're working to with the architect, that the building does not depend solely on artificial lighting, or that it doesn't depend solely on air conditioning. A building can work without those systems but it depends upon where in the world you're working.

For a project in the U.K. outside Cambridge, the climate is variable. Therefore there isn't a single solution or snapshot piece of architecture. It is a piece of architecture associated with time. There's a period where the building is overheating, and there's a period where the building is getting too cool. And there's a period where the outside conditions are ideal to the inside conditions where you prefer not to have a building at all. So working on buildings with architects, we work with things called "planned depths". We work with architects talking about "thermal mass". We talk about natural forces.

The natural forces of gravity, the forces of air molecule movement or wind, and solar radiation; a huge spectrum. I am a structural and civil engineer, I deal

Guy Battle / Chris McCarthy
Battle/McCarthy Engineers

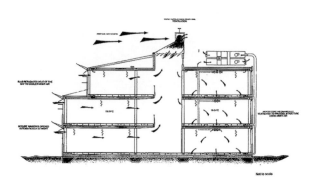

8.02 the concept of the air flow and stack ventilation. Ionica Building, Cambridge, UK engineered by Battle McCarthy. Architects, RH Partnership.

8.03 spanning the tracks: the complexity of the engineering solution, railway interchange, Kuala Lumpur

with physical things. But light is a fantastic subject in itself that starts off at 0.1 lux — whatever that means — to 100,000 lux. That's moonlight to bright sunlight. It's one to a million. Gravity is 9.81 meters per second squared; that's it, end of story. But there is a huge variety of light. Most of it has color. And therefore it's a subject in itself that is ever changing, ever worth exploring.

The other areas of exploration are the subjects of gravity, wind and solar radiation, not problems to be solved, but a mystery to be experienced. First we're going to discuss gravity. Now working with different architects there are often different needs. One of the areas that is a need is the shortage of land. Where is the land? Do you build over the next farmland? Or do you start to look at other sites such as railways, roads, and waterways to build over? The move is now to build over many of the existing infrastructures, to restitch the urban network. The principle of it is that it is land that can be regenerated. Not regenerated and re-earthed, but actually bridged over. The problem we're faced with is a simple one of taking gravity over a space. And we're talking large-scale spaces; we're talking 50, 200 meter spans in certain cases. One case is the railway just south of Kuala Lumpur. You have three railways. You have the KTM, the LRT, and the RL. But what is important is that these three railways come together. Where they come together it is also associated with the orbital ring road. The planning policy of Kuala

Lumpur is to stop cars coming into the city. Therefore they need to build an interchange where cars terminate, and then from that spot you change to another mode of transportation to get on to the train that then takes you to the city, or to the airport, or to take the train to Bangkok or Singapore.

So the areas of interchange are becoming very interesting, very complex, and extremely important. We are after all, all disabled, we need machines to carry us. As engineers working now on the subject of gravity there is a formulation of the structural grid, an understanding of different systems, and then we look at the different elements. That is the sort of conversation that's continued from the beginning of the whole concept of structural design. So working on those principles we start to look at different options of spanning the railway. There are infinite options. An excitement about working with architects is that you're exploring the creation of different options that need to be tested. Tested for efficiency, for cost, for buildability.

With two options we developed you can support the building at low level, or you can actually increase the depth of the structure by accommodating space within the building. By doing that, once you increase the depth, you can then remove the number of supports that you have, and then you can make savings in the ground. But what's the issue here? The issue here is that there is variety, there is choice, there is a fam-

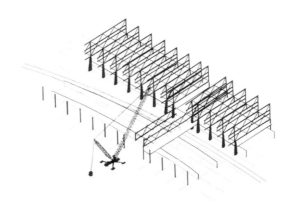

8.04 the structural columns at the core of the Regional government offices, Marseilles. William Alsop Architects

8.05 engineering the construction sequence: railway interchange, Kuala Lumpur

ily of options that can be developed, and then each of those options can be tested. Too often we have single answers being looked for instead of stepping back and looking at options. Now from those options you can then generate the best of the options. We will never produce the best building, ever. It's just the best of the options at the time. It's a bit boring to watch a horse race with one horse, so we really enjoy the idea that in design you actually create options. The final option in this particular case was to place the supporting structure within the car park grid. The fact is we know what car parks look like. We know the layouts of car parks. To place a structure within, say, retail space that's forever changing in need, wouldn't have been suitable.

When designing and developing structures you end up with a grid and the elements. Simultaneously, you are thinking of the actual sections you are working with. In dealing with spanning thousands upon thousands of tons of load over existing and future railways, the steel sections are not going to be the typical steel sections you associate with construction. The sections that this particular building used are flanges five inches deep. So the elements are small; they're compact. And because they're small and compact they have an inherent fire resistance. They're like a huge kettle to heat up, and thus they don't require fire protection. So you've made another saving in this ever-improving efficiency of the overall design.

Now, as architects, you become very interested in the finished form. In reality, the "gravity of importance", or the "structure of importance", is during construction. Bridges are designed for their construction, not for their final forces. And from the concept stage, it is important to bring on board the people that are actually going to build it — the structural engineers should be consultants. We create the design, but we're not the person that's going to actually build it. As an example, there are 1,000 ton cranes that can lift 300 tons of steel 30 meters away, and place it. So the design itself has to accommodate that. But you can imagine that each of the trusses weighs something like 2,000 tons each. So you can't actually lift a single truss. So a "crisscross" truss idea was developed so that you only had to lift half a truss at a time. The other thing you can do is push them out. You literally fabricate them on one side, and just push out the actual elements. But the chosen solution was a travelling method. And this process is whereby you construct a temporary platform upon which' you fabricate the trusses at one end, and you just push them out. And it's fascinating that we are not only talking about design efficiency, but also speed erection. As the trusses are being pushed out, and they're being fitted out. The floors are being laid and air conditioning is being installed.

Guy Battle:
One of the things that we're beginning to do as an engineering practice is communicate through analy-

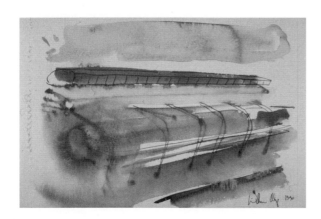

8.06 watercolour painting by William Alsop of the Marseilles project

8.07 sectional elevation of "Big Blue", Marseilles. William Alsop Architects

sis. Some of the very visual analysis forms that are now available actually help an architect understand what they are producing. I think architects don't use enough communication in a graphical form, actually imagining what a space is going to be like in terms of light, heat, sound, and movement; and then painting it, or drawing it, or communicating it. Most architects actually don't understand the environment they're trying to create. They know that "this is the form and shape and ultimately a lux level is a lux level". But as Chris McCarthy pointed out, a lux level is dependenton whether it comes from the north, south, east or west — it has different color renderings and different qualities. I really believe that architects must communicate with engineers so that we can fully understand what they are trying to achieve with spaces.

One of the beauties about working with William Alsop on a competition for a town hall in Marseilles, France, is that he really gives us that help in this sort of visual form. The fascinating thing about Marseilles, as a climatic environmental engineer, is the difference between Southern France and the United Kingdom. Initially when we designed this building seven years ago, we didn't realize the difference would be so great. And the differences come not only in physiological factors in terms of the temperatures we have to achieve in the building, or light levels, but it comes in the cultural interpretation of those comfort levels. I recall a song entitled, "On

the Sunny Side of the Street". In the U.K. it actually isn't that sunny that often, and you want to walk in the sun; it's great to walk in the sun. Whereas in Marseilles, don't walk on the sunny side of the street because you are going to boil. Get on the shady side of the street, wear sunglasses. As a result, the way we designed the atrium space was not to be a big open space with lots of light coming into it. It needed to be a selected shading system, something that filtered the light. In terms of light again: we went down to one of our first design team meetings, and it was quite late in the afternoon. The sun was coming straight into the window, the blinds were pulled down, and it was about 200 lux on the desk — quite a low level. I was thinking there's not enough light. But because the light was associated with heat and overheating, that was the comfortable light level. In the U.K. you would never dream of specifying 200 lux in summer. You'd be specifying 400 or 500 lux because that is what you need to work.

So all these different factors came into play in the design of the building. In terms of the general form of a building, part of it was an idea by Will Alsop in terms of him wanting a strong shape. But we helped form that shape in terms of the local environment. The mistral is an extremely strong wind, it's a way of life. When the wind is blowing during certain times of the year, people batten down the hatches. They expect it; it is a way of living. And the building tried to take on that same response. One of the key

8.08 structural detail of the roof and awning of the *Deliberatif,* Marseilles.

8.09 the intereior of the public atrium to the *Administratif* at Marseilles.

factors that we had with the building was the north-west facade and the wind. The mistral hits the facade and creates a cycling of air down onto the square. So we ended up having to design a wind shelf to force the wind around the square.

The other aspect, in terms of air movement, is that of the atrium space. The atrium space is about light, but it's also about air movement to create a stack effect to drive the air up through the building. The idea was to create narrow streets rather than very wide streets, so the light would be filtered down. In terms of the analysis that we carried out, we looked very carefully at the ventilation, the air movement through the space, and went through a whole series of analyses, not only during the summertime. The analyses showed air coming in at a low level,   forcing its way across the floor, and then moving up out of the building driven by a stack effect. During the wintertime what we were having was a cycling down of air movement. In the end we designed an underfloor heating system to reduce the air movement at low level; it was causing discomfort. But it is only a very low level of heating at about 10 degrees centigrade. It's not an internal conservatory as such, but that helped us understand the nature of the space, and the nature of the air movement in the space.

We are also designing a very different building in Brussels. It is a stand alone building you could say, but it's in a city center. The challenge in this particular building which is an existing structure is to give it a new life, to refurbish it. We worked with architects Kohn Pedersen Fox, in their London office, who are beginning to develop some quite sustainable or low energy approaches to architecture.

One of the key problems we had on this particular building that we had to maintain for planning reasons was the low floor to floor height. It's mostly residential at present, but we needed to change it into office space. And it needed to be an office space that could be let to the European Union who had quite stiff requirements in terms of temperature control and daylighting. But the floor to floor height is only 3.1 meters. Yet they wanted it fully air conditioned and daylit. So rather than sending all our services through the center of the building, we designed a double skin. A skin outside the building contains all the services and also acts as the solar control system. We had the very long facades facing the worst directions where you have low angle sun which was proving to be a real problem. So the creation of a double skin actually allows us to filter out the worst effect of the solar radiation. But during the wintertime allows us to use it as a massive collector. So it is in fact a solar control system during the summertime, but also a solar collector during the wintertime. The whole idea is about a chameleon skin, an intelligent skin, something that is actually thinking. The chameleon is a creature that adapts to its envi-

Guy Battle / Chris McCarthy
Battle/McCarthy Engineers

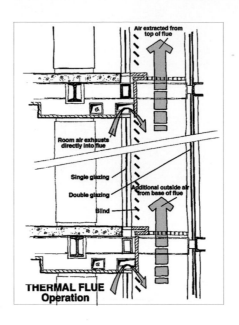

8.10 model of renovated building with integrated wind turbine: International Rogiere building, Brussels. Architects Kohn Pedersen Fox.

8.11 the ideas of the external wall and the thermal flue: International Rogiere building, Brussels

ronment — summer to winter — and to different forms of local environments — woody to jungle or whatever. Buildings should be adaptable as well. It shouldn't just be a static object that sets itself for one season — it should be a compromise between all seasons. It should change according to season, and indeed between night and day, and between different uses. And this intelligent skin would have to regulate energy flow through itself whether it's in to out, or out to in,and store any excess energy that it doesn't need immediately. And then either redistribute this excess energy to areas of the building or areas of the city where it is required, or dissipate it in some form.

In terms of the light radiation aspects that we were dealing with, we were faced with a fait accompli; a deep plan building of 16 meters. So inevitably there is a central section that just can't receive any daylight, so that area is going to have artificial light the whole time. Our real task was to ensure that the perimeter zones of about 4.5 meters were daylit for as long as it is actually physically possible. And so we have achieved a daylight space for something like 70% of the year which we think is quite acceptable. And we achieved it by having plenty of glazing on the outside of the building. Now, the problem with glazing, especially on the east and west facade is that you get all the associated solar gain.

So the next challenge was to say "How do we control the solar radiation that comes in with the lighting to actually keep the heat out of the building?" The glazing system is as follows. You have an inner single glaze. You have a blind on the outer face of that single glazing. Then we have an outer double glazing system. The air is supplied from air handling units at the top of the building using ductwork that runs within this double skin, supplying air into the building. We have chilled beams within the building itself. The air then is naturally drawn out of the building, and partly through stack effects. Eventually it is recirculated via air handling units, and heat reclaim units at the top of the building. During the summertime this hot air is just thrown directly away because we can't reuse the heat. But during the wintertime the air is then used to recycle. Now this is what is so fascinating about the design as we went through it. We spent a lot of time looking at this double skin because the whole architecture is hung on the double skin. As an environmental engineer I found that absolutely terrifying because usually I am designing ductwork. Now if you under-design the fans, you can put a bigger fan in; take the duct out, change it. It's not the end of the world. If a structure falls down, that's the end of the world; that's serious. But on this building the ductwork is on the outside of the building. In fact, I am using the double skin. I'm using the architecture as my ductwork. Suddenly we had to understand that level of responsibility — and do a lot of analysis to prove that it was going to work.

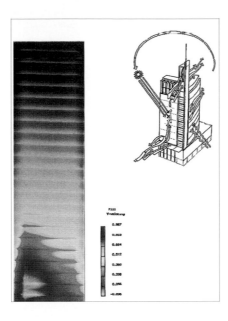
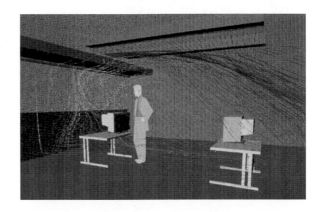

8.12 simulating the wind velocities around the enclosure: International Rogiere building, Brussels

8.13 computational fluid dynamic (CFD) simulation of air movement in office space: International Rogiere building, Brussels

Guy Battle / Chris McCarthy
Battle/McCarthy Engineers

We spent a lot of time using CFD, computational fluid dynamic analysis, looking at the minutest of details. The difference between the blind being on this side, and being on that side. The distance between the two glazings. It is actually 1.2 meters. But it made a big difference whether it was 1.2 or .9 meters. There was a massive difference between this blind being on the inner face, or the outer face. Now initially as an engineer I was saying "We've got to put it on the outer face." "It makes no sense," you would say, "because the heat's kept on the outside." and indeed that was where we wanted to put it. But the architect said "We just can't make it work. It's really difficult to have your blind control system, and it's automatic, out here, and it looks ugly. Can you just test it for us on the inner face?"

What happens is that the cool air is extracted, it goes through a hole in a facade. Because it's cooler than the air in the double skin, it actually drops down in between the blind and the inner glaze, and creates another buffer zone. So it is actually doing a double job. Not only is this blind cutting out the solar radiation as it's coming into the building, but actually it's forming a cool furnace around the outside of each glazing system. So glass, rather than being up to 40 degrees centigrade is actually at room temperature. It means the radiant temperature in the space is extremely low, and extremely efficient. And even when we don't have the blind in use it still works well because for fire reasons we had to have an over-

hang of a meter to prevent fire jump from floor to floor.

Another aspect of the International Rogiere as it's known in Brussels is that we wanted to push it as an example of sustainability within cities — or a building that not only collects but also produces energy. A feature of high-rise buildings is that at the very top it's very windy, as you expect. And yet so often there's no advantage taken of that wind, it's usually just ignored. Velocity increases exponentially, but the beauty of the power output from a turbine is related to velocity cubed. You only have to double the velocity, and you actually cube the power output of your turbine. So that gives you a lot of advantage on high-rise buildings, and is an ideal resource. Now you could claim "Why have wind turbines in cities?" Well, the argument is that if you've got them in the countryside, they create visual pollution. At least in a city it's cluttered, it's full of everything that creates a city and it's where the energy is needed. Why have turbines out in the middle of the countryside when you need your energy in the city and subsequently have to transport it from the countryside, with all the associated costs?

This was the solution. Air is caught on the southwest facade, then forced up and through the turbine. It's going to contribute roughly 10% of the building's energy use, which is not massive, but it's not insignificant. The client is interested in pursuing it and

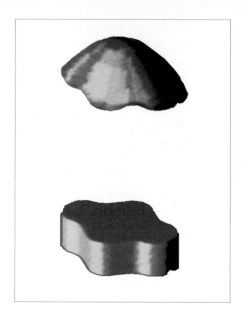

8.14 sketch of the wind pressures and air flow through the energy generating turbine: International Rogiere building, Brussels

8.15 finding the efficiency of forms: through the process of transformation using the natural forces of gravity, air molecule movement, wind or solar radiation.

indeed the planners are supporting it as well.

We have discussed gravity, air movement, wind, and radiation. But we believe there is someone missing from the design team. There is a challenge that we would like to lay down to architects and to MIT. The first is to understand the brief, to understand that architecture must be a response to climate, to see how the climate actually forms that architecture, especially in the U.S. with its diverse climate zones. And secondly to understand the natural forces that exist in terms of radiation, air movement or wind, and gravity, seeing how those things can be manipulated, can be used to find form in the architecture so that architecture isn't only about art, it's actually about a physical response to its environment.

Battle McCarthy has been carrying out studies on trying to find "optimal forms". We took a standard form, and we tried to optimize it in terms of gravity, in terms of air movement, in terms of internal radiation, in terms of sound, and various other factors. Trying to look and see what is the optimum shape, what is the optimum form that an understanding of those forces would take. You end up with a number of different ideal forms, each optimized for a certain force. There is an ideal form for gravity, an ideal for radiation, an ideal for air movement, etc. Then we amalgamated all the forms. Now, this is not architecture as we know it today by any means, and we're certainly not saying that this is the solution, nor are

these necessarily the answers to the individual forces. But it's the process that is very important. The process of the understanding of the forces, and allowing the architecture to respond to those forces.

The input of the material sciences is a dimension we want to explore with architects and students. Do not work with concrete, steel, and types of glasses, work with notions of stiffness, of thermal capacity, of heat resistance, of transparency and translucency. Work with the actual physics. Understand the physics that you require for your building for the internal environment you're trying to meet. Then work with a materials scientist, and say "Look, I need this material here with this specification. Can you design it with me? Can you design it for me?" If we move in that direction, and build the materials up from a molecular atomic level then we really have an opportunity to discover a new way forward, a new architecture for the 21st century.

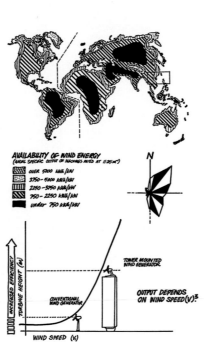

8.16 the availability and efficiency of wind generation

8.17 the poetics of integrating form, structure and engineering

David Richards
Ove Arup & Partners, Engineers

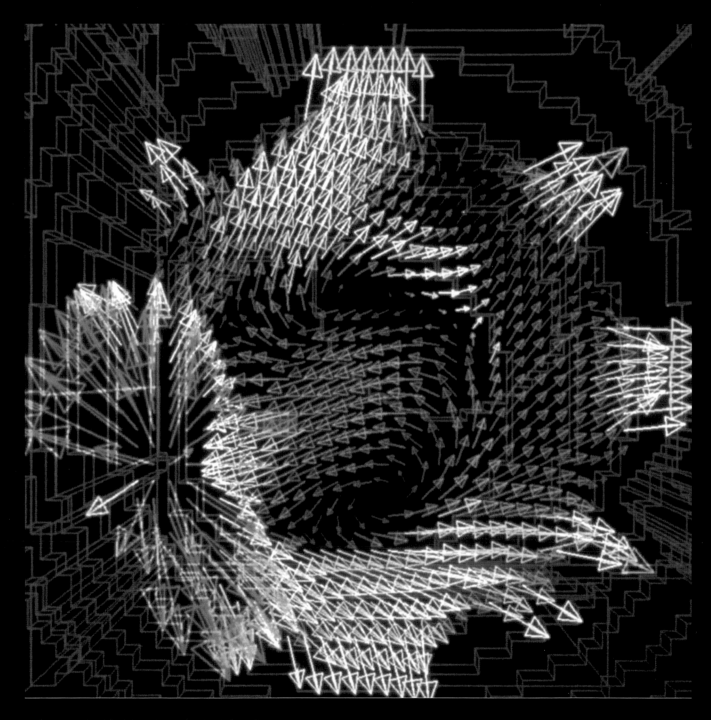

9.00 computational fluid dynamics model (CFD): Sony Center,
Potsdamer Platz, Berlin

Concept to Demolition: An Integrated Approach to Sustainability

David Richards
Ove Arup & Partners, Engineers
New York, U.S.A.

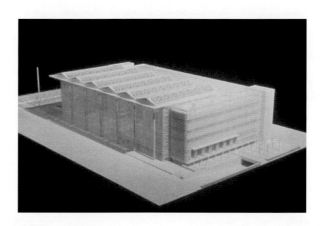

9.01 model of Phoenix Federal Courthouse and the atrium: Richard Meier and Partners.

In terms of sustainability, the work at Ove Arup's generally falls into two areas. There are issues we naturally deal with as part of the usual design process, that fall within the framework of our usual scope, and there are projects where we are asked to solve a particular, more involved problem. I will discuss a few of these special projects first, offer some broad conclusions, and then discuss a few more practical issues about how we work in the U.S.

The first project is the Phoenix Courthouse, a new building in Arizona. We are working with Richard Meier specifically on the design of the atrium, a space of about 400 by 150 feet in plan and 6 storeys tall, with entire glazed surfaces facing north and east and a glazed roof. The principle is to create a feeling of open public space that Phoenix lacks due to its aggressive climate. Clearly it is a high heat gain space. The traditional approach would be to throw cold air at it, which is not sustainable. To be convinced of the benefits, the client needed to be convinced that heavy air conditioning and increased energy use and running costs could be avoided.

The first point to appreciate about Phoenix is the very hot and dry climate. The outdoor conditions in 1990, which we chose to use as our design year, was a very hot year in the U.S. The climate in Phoenix falls below 40% humidity for a large proportion of the year, meaning that the air has a great capacity to absorb water that we could exploit with evaporative cooling. Evaporative cooling uses a similar mechanism to perspiration from the human body. In the same way the human body is cooled by evaporating sweat, evaporating water cools air.

We made an hour by hour analysis to draw out more accurate statistics. We found that the outdoor temperature in Phoenix exceeds 73 degrees Fahrenheit for about 2/3 of the year, and reaches a high of 122 degrees Fahrenheit, which is very hot! With evaporative cooling, we found that for about 60% of the year we could bring the atrium down within the range of 68 degrees to 77degrees Fahrenheit. For a further 15% of the year we could keep it from 77 to 87degrees. We were above 87 degrees for about 2% of the year, around 70 hours a year. The temperature rarely gets much above 96 degrees Fahrenheit. These figures sound high, but in Phoenix they are not if you consider that the atrium is acting as a transition zone for people that are outside in 122 degrees Fahrenheit heat, coming inside where the rest of the building is air conditioned to around 75 degrees Fahrenheit. So, with some statistical proof, we could bring these temperatures within acceptable ranges.

From there, we moved on to design a system that would actually make this process work. We first took a simplified model of the atrium, and ran an analysis

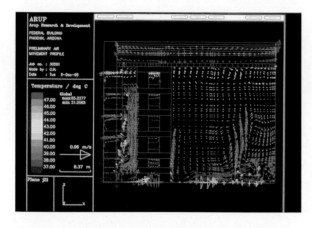

9.02 simulating the evaporative cooling of the atrium. Phoenix Federal Courthouse: Richard Meier and Partners.

9.03 the form of the Forum: Sony center, Berlin. Murphy Jahn Architects

program to get surface temperatures. From surface temperatures we moved through to CFD studies - computational fluid dynamics. Our first step was to model the input of air at low level and some open areas where we let air flow out at a high level. This gave some interesting results. We were following the intuitive approach to let the air in at low level, allow it rise due to buoyancy and escape at high level. The top of the Atrium is the thermal driver that captures the sun's heat to drive the stack effect. We found that this wasn't very stable. It didn't work very well because the air we were introducing at low level was being cooled by evaporation which meant it was heavy, dense air that wanted to stay at the base of the atrium. The stack effect wasn't strong enough to overcome this, which resulted in unstable cycling.

The second problem we confronted was located at the edge of the atrium where there are some balconies. The idea with these was simply to condition them with the spill air from the rest of thebuilding. But that wasn't working very well either. The highest balcony was approaching 122degrees Fahrenheit. It was this second problem that led to the solution to the first.

We looked at ways we could create a more comfortable microclimate on the balcony by air conditioning, to supplement the spill air to achieve comfortable temperatures. That was fine, but we then had to find a way of getting a separation here between the

microclimate and the atrium. One way was to place a piece of glass there, which wasn't acceptable architecturally. The other alternative was to use an air curtain. That led us to think about how we could solve the fighting airflows in the atrium. The solution we designed was to introduce the evaporative cooling at the top corner. With this approach we would get a down draft of cool air which would sink to the bottom of the atrium, forming a pool down in the occupied zone. By virtue of this velocity an air curtain was created, separating the balcony from the atrium. The air then escapes at a low level. So the buoyancy forces are counte- intuitive, which is interesting. We found that the temperatures in the space were satisfactory. As you would expect they were very high up at the top, comfort was achieved on the Balconies, and a good comfort range resulted down below. Eventually for architectural reasons the water sprayers were placed above the top balcony; air actually tracks along underneath the shading device. Some air is drawn into the shades and escapes.

Ove Arup and Partners have also been working on Potsdamer Platz in the heart of Berlin, a group of buildings for Sony which have a forum at their center. It has a wonderful roof over it — an offset conical structure made from steel with fabric and glass panels. We were involved in studying the environment in the forum. The client wanted to know if it was an occupiable, and consequently lettable, space.

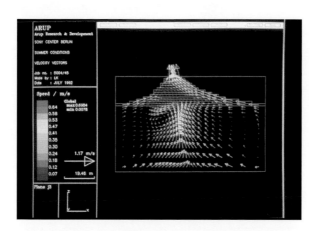

9.04 simulatiing the environmental performance of the Forum space: Sony Center, Berlin.

9.05 lighting simulation of office space overlooking the Forum, using Radiance software. Sony Center, Berlin.

The goals of our study were predicting thermal comfort in the space, confirming that there would be enough daylight in the forum and in the spaces that looked into it and to use the results to guide the facade design. We also carried out some acoustic and smoke simulations. The network of analyses was by no means simple.

Our first step was to look at daylight in the forum. We used the lighting simulation program Radiance to generate wonderful, photo-realistic images, as well as good technical data. Having studied the forum space we found that lighting levels were very good at the base of the forum — 3,000 to 4,000 lux under a uniform cloudy sky. We then looked at the office spaces that overlooked the forum. Under the same overcast sky, lighting levels on the desktop are in the order of 300 to 400 lux, which is perfectly adequate for a general light level in an office. We then went on to do some CFD studies. These told us that we get a wonderful throughdraft in summer and buoyant air escaping through the apex of the roof.

Having established the natural ventilation rates in the forum we then looked at comfort. Relative to outdoor conditions the forum is more comfortable for a number of reasons: it is heated by heat lost from surrounding buildings, it is shielded from the chilling effects of the wind and the roof reduces radiation losses. Our analysis confirmed these effects. We

sliced the results up in a few different ways. For most daylight hours the forum meets thermal comfort standards, certainly more than outside. And for the hours from noon to midnight, about 80% of those hours are comfortable. For the client these were the important hours because they were looking to stage concerts and to rent the space for cafeteria and commercial space. So again by careful analysis we could show the client that they now had additional space for which they didn't have to pay higher energy bills and didn't have to put up too much extra structure to create.

However, we should be cautious when jumping to the use of computer software. On the daylight studies for Kansai Airport in Japan, we showed that whilst computer analysis is a fantastic tool, it is not the only way. In this case we carried out physical modelling. By just building a model and putting it under an artificial sky, or just under even office lighting, you can support the idea of the design; physical models are far more flexible and intuitive than computer models. Computer models also take too long to be used quickly in the concept stage of a project. At the early stages this was the way we worked. In fact, on Kansai Airport it was the only way we worked. The models allowed us to optimize skylights in the main terminal building. We could reduce the HVAC and lighting energy consumption by something like 11%. Unfortunately, the client decided that they didn't want the headache of skylights despite the

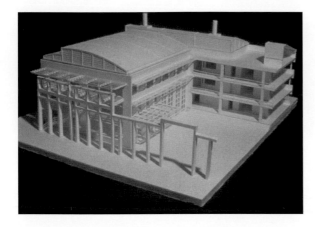

9.06 model: National University of Science and Technology, Bulawayo, Zimbabwe. Davis Brody Bond Architects

9.07 model showing the end of the glass atrium: Phoenix Federal Courthouse. Richard Meier and Partners.

energy savings. Maintenance, I guess, was a major issue there. They did not put them in, which was a shame.

It is not uncommon to lose seemingly viable energy saving measures through the design process. For the National University of Science and Technology in Bulawayo, Zimbabwe we designed the master planning and competition scheme with architects Davis Brody. It is important to understand that Zimbabwe has an absolutely beautiful climate, it doesn't get too hot, and it doesn't get too cold. Locally, another issue to understand is that they don't have very good power. It's very expensive and unreliable. We were trying to build laboratory buildings in a location where power is uncertain. We worked with Davis Brody to develop a language of very open buildings, integrating shading with the external circulation routes to limit solar gain and incorporating thermal mass to dampen internal gains. We explored a number of schemes with thermal mass trying to find the optimum solution for both climate control and cost. Initially we looked at a flat slab. That worked very well, but used a lot of concrete. We investigated a coffered scheme. That worked well but was expensive to form. The optimum solution ended up being precast Ts, which provided adequate thermal mass with a large exposed surface area and were relatively cheap. Having established these key elements we found that we had some buildings that did not need any cooling, or even need any heating; the ultimate

passive buildings.

Things began to unravel when the design was handed over to local consultants in Zimbabwe — two things happened. Firstly, the client came under pressure from a local aluminium-cladding contractor to use their product. Secondly, the client became convinced that what they wanted was a building with a Western image, which meant a glass building with suspended ceilings, and this wasn't it. So in their effort to aspire to Western culture they lost the passive effects.

I will return to the Phoenix courthouse briefly to talk about glass. The Courthouse is undoubtedly a very elegant building, which we matched with an elegant technical solution to the problem. I have two problems with this scheme. First, whilst it is a low energy solution it does use a lot of water in cooling the air by evaporation. I am not sure that is really very sustainable. It can be explained away because it still uses no more than a regular cooling tower scheme would have used and with a far lower energy input. But the more fundamental issue is to ask whether the premise of the problem was sustainable. We were, after all, putting a glass box in the middle of the desert. Not only were the heat gains enormous but glass as a material is very energy-intensive to produce, and not recyclable to vision quality glass. The use of large areas of glass in buildings is a very common theme. Recently a common way to limit its

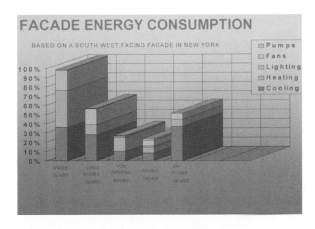

FACADE ENERGY CONSUMPTION

9.08 comparative energy analysis of facade constructions: Ove Arup and Partners

9.09 photovoltaic energy generating facade renovation, as seen from the inside: Kiss Cathcart Architects

detrimental effect on energy consumption has been to use double or ventilated facades. I believe their use is highly questionable.

Let me take a simplified look at how double facades came about. Imagine you start with a piece of glass — a full height single-glazed window. It doesn't work very well. It lets too much heat in; it lets too much heat out. So you double-glaze it. That works a bit better but it still allows a lot of energy to flow in and out and may not meet all the energy codes it needs to. So it needs shading on it. Shading works best on the outside so the shading goes on the outside. That doesn't look so great so another sheet of glass is introduced to give it a more unified appearance. This is a double facade but it has some heat trapped in the cavity. The trapped heat can reduce the overall performance and anyway the excess heat can be used to heat the building. So the facade becomes ventilated — probably naturally in summer and sometimes mechanically acting as the buildings fresh air pre-heater in winter and mid seasons. Now the facade is described as energy saving. In reality that may not be the case. A bar chart shows some typical figures. They are relatively crude and for a specific orientation and location, but they do illustrate the point. A double facade does not compare that favorably. A simple facade with a relatively low glazing ratio can still give adequate daylight, especially with the use of light shelves. It will be a facade that probably has a lower embodied energy, and at least com-

parable running costs and energy consumption. Let us not jump to the complex solution too quickly or claim that it is sustainable when it may not be.

A more interesting development of glass that we are involved in is photovoltaics. A project that we worked on with Gregory Kiss, a New York architect, began life as an entry to an AIA idea competition for building-integrated photovoltaics in which Andrew Scott was a fellow winner. The challenge we set ourselves was an existing building we knew of in Hamburg that had a facade that had been performing very poorly. It leaked a lot, and it was very uncomfortable. We proposed to drape a second skin over that facade rather than replace it. It gave us a number of benefits. It reduced wind pressure on the facade — hence lowering infiltration of outdoor air — and it reduced solar gain. The cavity we created in this case could also be used for fresh air intake, reclaiming the high heat dissipation of photovoltaics. Our analysis suggested that it reduces the cooling load by 20% and the heating load by 15%. Added to this, it creates new space in the atrium and has a longer period for occupancy than the existing terrace. Our proposal was to create a double facade of sorts but in this case it was driven by the poor performance of an existing building and resulted in a more comfortable building, using less energy and creating additional space.

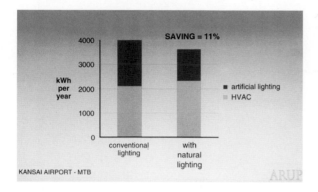

9.10 the effect of daylighting upon energy consumption at Kansai Airport: Ove Arup and Partners.

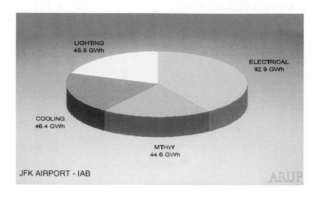

9.11 annual energy consumption at JFK Airport, New York, International Arrivals building: Ove Arup and Partners

The phases of building in construction, operation, and maintenance are where I am convinced we should be starting to move to have the most effect. We have many tools available to design energy efficient buildings. What is less common, certainly in the United States, is to be able to run a building energy efficiently. The JFK Terminal, the International Arrival Building at New York, was built in the '50s and was built to standards that were current at that time. It's not particularly efficient. The point to appreciate about an airport is that it has to exist in a very aggressive climate. A few of the factors to bear in mind with an airport, regardless of where it is in the world, are it has to deal with noise, pollution and the fact that at times there are large numbers of people in it, so it has very high internal gains. Usually, they are also quite deep plan buildings, which make natural ventilation difficult.

Ove Arup took a look at the buildings systems as part of the building analysis we were doing with architects SOM. The client knew it wasn't working well and they wanted to know why. We found that it was consuming something like 230 gigawatt hours a year of energy, which sounds unbelievably big. It comes out in the order of $14 to 15 million a year running cost. We found that most of their air conditioning systems were "constant volume". They were delivering the same volume of air into a space regardless of what the heat load was and just varied the temperature of the air to meet the load. On the

whole they were running 24 hours a day regardless of occupancy patterns. The lights were generally on 24 hours a day regardless of daylight conditions or occupancy. There was some large-scale energy wastage.

We looked at passenger flow as a start point. Passenger volumes vary enormously in an airport - take for example a baggage carousel. The HVAC systems were sized with the assumption that the maximum number of people were in there all the time. Fresh air for all those people was supplied all day and night, which means that they're heating and cooling air that they really don't need to. When we looked at it more closely, working with NAPA, the airport planning specialists, we found that the real HVAC peak was substantially lower than anticipated. That told us two things. Firstly, a variable air volume system would be far more efficient. It would work by varying the air volume against the load in the space and saving significant fan energy. Secondly, if the quality of the air in the space was measured and the amount of fresh air limited to maintain good quality, they could reduce their heating and cooling energy consumption quite considerably.

We also looked at daylight saving measures. For example, changing the circuiting of the lights so they could be switched with the changing daylight levels adjacent to windows. We also looked for situations where entire areas of the building could be shut

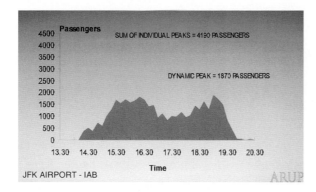

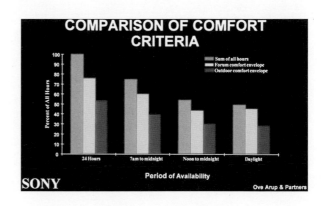

9.12 fluctuations in the occupancy of the baggage reclaim area: JFK Airport, New York, International Arrivals building: Ove Arup and Partners

9.13 where does the comfort come from?: Sony Center, Berlin

down when they were empty. For example overnight or, in the case of gate lounges, just when they didn't have a flight operating out of them. All in all we predicted that they could save in the order of 70% of the energy they were consuming.

Eventually this proved to be a moot point. For other more fundamental operating reasons they decided their interests were best served by demolishing the existing terminal and rebuilding. This leads to a number of issues where as a profession we are still not very sophisticated. Going into existing buildings we frequently see poorly maintained equipment, working inefficiently, wasting energy. As designers perhaps we should be getting more involved in how building operators go about maintaining these buildings. We should be designing buildings that can be maintained and perhaps going as far as writing the specification for maintaining the building. At the moment that responsibility falls to the contractor but because of the way we compartmentalize the design process, the contractor has no interest in running the building. Their job is simply to deliver the building. Responsibility then moves on to the maintenance team who are probably underfunded by the client and who can't maintain the building properly. So no matter how much energy efficiency is designed into the building it can be greatly diminished through lack of proper maintenance.

We need to find a way of cementing the whole

process. I would be keen to see a way of exciting the entire building community towards sustainability so that designers, builders, operators and clients all have an interest in buildings designed to be low energy. Bill Browning and the Rocky Mountain Institute are doing work on performance-related fees which is a positive move.

We should also revisit our attitude to refurbishment. Take a fan for example. The standard attitude in a refurbishment is to replace it with a new one. Often when a piece of equipment like a fan is replaced it is replaced with an almost identical technology — fans haven't advanced. So why bother replacing it? Why not refurbish it? Why isn't the manufacturer able to take this stuff back, refurbish it and give it back for reinstallation. A parallel is a photocopier in Europe. Oce are now designing their machines to be taken back when they finish their useful life. They strip them down, reuse and recycle as much as they can, and waste as little as possible. As much as 60% of the components are reused, 35% are recycled and only 5% thrown away. 5% too much I guess. But we could apply that principle to many, many building components. We have to start trying to persuade manufacturers to start thinking like that.

Another area we should revisit is building codes. In a project we are working on with Richard Meier, a house in Florida, we had to deal with the Florida

9.14 model of Neugeberger House, Naples, Florida: Richard Meier and Partners.

State Energy Code. It's about an inch and a half thick and comes with its own computer software. Any building design is fed into the program. The program gives a score and if it is fewer than 100 you are "satisfactory". It is incredibly prescriptive and is not written as a guide to help you design but more as a set of rules that you must simply follow. This is fairly typical of U.S. codes, but needs to change. Codes should be broad technical guides that offer the opportunity to develop unusual solutions or to follow prescriptive methods. They should start with something that tells you what the spirit and the intent of the code is. They should then move on to maybe a prescriptive method that is easy. And they should finish with a much more intensive analysis method where you can prove that you meet the target of the code with innovative solutions. The new ASHRAE standard 90.1, is far more like that. I hope that it gets adopted more widely.

I would like to try and deal with a slightly more difficult subject. I get the impression that people often feel that in Europe there is more experience and knowledge of building low energy buildings. One of the reasons is that research and practice are far more interlinked in Europe than they are in the United States. When Ove Arup and Partners first arrived in New York we found that as much as we wanted to design very energy efficient buildings it was quite hard to justify the time to do it. So we looked in a little detail at what was different. Costs are very different in the United States. Broadly, engineers command higher salaries in the U.S., overheads are slightly lower, the working year is a little longer. Factoring all this in we found that in the U.K., engineers have three times as many hours to design than they do in the U.S. In the U.K., people have more time to do research while they're practicing, which makes an enormous difference not only to the quality of design but also to the strength of links between industry and research. Conversely, the lack of fees in the U.S. tends to drive consultants to a more formulaic approach — hence the reduction of codes to rulebooks rather than guides for good practice to be exceeded by thoughtful design.

So, some key issues for the future. We need to continue doing integrated and sustainable design using appropriate analysis tools. Let's start persuading manufacturers to reuse. Let's try and bring research and practice much closer together. And let's get paid to do this work because otherwise I am afraid it will be very difficult to make it happen, especially in the commercial sector. I guess you can summarize that with this definition of green: buildings that are designed, constructed and demolished in an environmentally enhanced way.

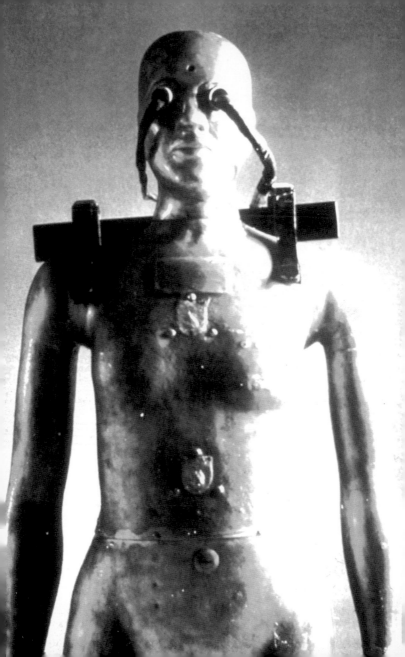

Architecture Revisited: On Listening to Buildings

Charles C. Benton
University of California at Berkeley
Berkeley, California, U.S.A.

10.01 as the elephant was to the wise blind men, so architecture is to us

Architects establish in their designs a frame for our daily lives. A frame that reflects culture, region, and place. A frame that shapes our well being as building occupants and establishes global patterns of energy use. We face a paradox of sorts. We know more about the physical performance of buildings than at any other point in history. We have extraordinary tools like computational fluid dynamics to inform design. We have exceptional capacities at hand in materials, processes, and environmental control systems. For instance, we deposit invisible layers of metal on glass, and fine tune their properties within fine tolerances to control the transmission of specific electromagnetic wavelengths. Energy to run buildings is available in unprecedented quantity and it is still relatively inexpensive in the United States. Yet with all of this capacity, contemporary buildings somehow manage to perform poorly and often disappoint their occupants. This talk examines the physical performance paradox and describes the Vital Signs Project, a curriculum materials initiative addressing its treatment in architectural education.

The United States is home to something in the order of 4.5% of the world's population. We consume over 24% of the world's energy, mostly through the combustion of fossil fuels. Of this embarrassingly hefty portion of the global pie, about 38% of US energy goes into buildings and building-housed processes, into shaping our interior environments. This is energy spent principally for lighting, cooling, ventilating, and heating. US buildings are thus responsible for almost 10% of the world's energy use – a pattern shaped by designers. Furthermore, buildings are among the most long-lived physical artifacts that society produces. If one makes a shoddy washing machine or television set, it will be recycled after a decade or so, but buildings last for a very long time. Today's designs will be with us for many decades.

Our buildings simultaneously exist in several forms. On one hand are the conceptions of image and intention so central to discourse in our architecture schools, our journals, and other architectural fora. But on the other hand is the tangible nature of buildings as physical artifacts. And unfortunately as artifacts buildings and their systems are often quite clumsy. In the US, vast sums are expended for the routine functions lighting, cooling, ventilation, and heating. Better design could reduce this expense, reduce environmental damage, and produce more satisfied building occupants.

I've come to think that the greatest potential for change lies in the earliest stages of architectural design, in the conception, the stroke of the soft pencil. In that stroke a design is malleable, here the designer's knowledge shapes the eventual building. For example, a single stroke of the soft pencil can create 50 years of uncomfortable occupants and mandated mechanical cooling. Whoosh: 400 feet of west-facing glass goes the pencil. Months later, an

Charles C. Benton

University of California, Berkeley

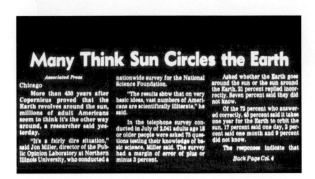

Many Think Sun Circles the Earth

Associated Press

Chicago

More than 450 years after Copernicus proved that the Earth revolves around the sun, millions of adult Americans seem to think it's the other way around, a researcher said yesterday.

"It's a fairly dire situation," said Jon Miller, director of the Public Opinion Laboratory at Northern Illinois University, who conducted a

nationwide survey for the National Science Foundation.

"The results show that on very basic ideas, vast numbers of Americans are scientifically illiterate," he said.

In the telephone survey conducted in July of 2,041 adults age 18 or older people were asked 75 questions testing their knowledge of basic science, Miller said. The survey had a margin of error of plus or minus 3 percent.

Asked whether the Earth goes around the sun or the sun around the Earth, 21 percent replied incorrectly. Seven percent said they did not know.

Of the 72 percent who answered correctly, 45 percent said it takes one year for the Earth to orbit the sun, 17 percent said one day, 2 percent said one month and 9 percent did not know.

The responses indicate that

Back Page Col. 4

10.02 We are increasingly removed from the sun's patterns

engineer determines that the building skin must be low transmitting glass – a strategy that compresses the richness of a building's relationship with nature into an assembly one inch or perhaps a quarter inch thick. Here heat-absorbing glass is selected to tame the unruly western sun and with that unfortunate decision the fate of the occupant is sealed. The heavily tinted glass blocks the sun with pigment, by absorbing it's energy. It's a strategy in which heat enters the building anyway through conduction but visible light does not. When exposed to the sun the window becomes hot to the touch. The thermal decisions wind up compromising the view outdoors, arguably one of the few amenities left in a sealed window. Occupants must shut their shades or blinds to keep the window's hot surface from causing thermal discomfort. Yet with all of these disadvantages, heat-absorbing glass is frequently used as a means of controlling solar gain. It is easy; an expediency. Ideally, architects should know the physical and experiential implications of their soft pencil strokes. If they did, heat-absorbing glass would be considerably less common.

Poor building performance is exacerbated by professional compartmentalization. These days rather elaborate teams come together to produce commercial buildings. Varying by project the teams are comprised of many specialists – surveyors, leasing agents, various engineering disciplines, architects, interior designers, and materials specialists. In com-

partmentalizing design procedures, the whole often gets lost. Each specialist comes to the design with their own agenda, their own measures of success, and their own way of speaking about things.

Let's take thermal comfort as an example. Are you comfortable now? Do you have cold feet? Ideally, buildings are designed to produce thermally comfortable interiors. Where do the specifications for comfort come from? In commercial buildings the HVAC engineer will design to ASHRAE's 55-92 Thermal Comfort Standard, which provides detailed specifications for the various combinations of air temperature, humidity, radiant surroundings, air velocity, clothing level, and activity level that should produce a comfortable human being. Those were derived, by and large, through laboratory experiments involving the physiology of humans and stated preference for comparative conditions in environmental control chambers. Experimental subjects, often college age students, were placed in the chambers and asked whether changes in the environment produced thermal conditions that were better or worse, colder or warmer. In some cases the studies eliminated the human subject altogether and used instead a thermal mannequin. Our research group at Berkeley has a hundred- thousand-dollar mannequin that has sixteen zones of skin. It's the most incredible environment sensor. It is a wonderful research tool.

The design of lighting in US commercial buildings is

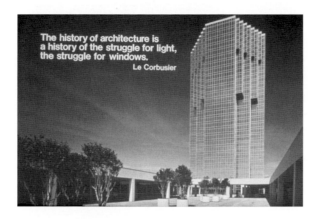

10.03 An unintentionally ironic title slide from a glass company presentation on daylighting

VITAL SIGNS	PROFILE
WHO?	The Building Science Group at U. C. Berkeley with sponsorship of the Energy Foundation, NSF, and Pacific Gas & Electric. Architecture faculty from over 20 other schools are involved.
WHAT?	A curriculum materials development project centered on student observation and measurement of the physical environment in existing buildings.
WHEN?	The project began in Jan. 1993 and is funded into 1999. Vital Signs activities will then continue under SBSE.
WHERE?	PG&E's Pacific Energy Center provides project offices and facilities.
WHY?	To encourage greater awareness of energy conservation techniques and their relationship with architectural spacemaking and occupant well-being.

10.04 The purpose of the Vital Signs project at University of California, Berkeley.

largely shaped by the standard practices of the Illuminating Engineering Society. We have an incredible palette of lighting sources, fixtures and controls available these days. In applying them the most common metric of lighting design is footcandles on a horizontal plane. This is in part because we can make an instrument that measures illuminance on a horizontal plane quite well while other measurements are more difficult. So interior lighting standards have evolved to refer to footcandles, our easily measured variable. Talk to any lighting designer, look at lighting designs, and you will find that illuminance as a metric is not particularly related to interior lighting quality. It does not communicate the quality and certainly not the magic of light. Illuminance simply reports an undifferentiated quantity of light striking an often abstract horizontal plane.

Daylight's rich variation, its strongest attribute, defies simple calculation and thus daylight is often neglected in design. Visit a US commercial building in the middle of the day when you have a bright 100,000-lux sky outside. In 99 out of 100 buildings, you'll see the lights running immediately next to the glazing. Though this is our standard practice it doesn't make much sense. I opened up the local newspaper the other day and read the headline "Many think sun circles the earth." I was horrified that they might be talking about our profession, about architects, and the fact that we have become so divorced from the sun. The sun is undeniably a driving force in our

buildings, a source of comfort and of potential pain.

The Libbey-Owens-Ford Glass Company begins a daylighting slide show with this quote from Le Corbusier: "The history of architecture is the history of the struggle for light, the struggle for windows". The quote is illustrated with a building in Atlanta named Plaza Towers. If ever a building struggled for light, this one does. It's clad with a very low (~5%) transmittance glass. Now glass is a wonderful, highly evolved material but this all-glass design lacks many of the basic amenities of a window. The deficit occurs at personal and operational levels. Perceptually, it is always overcast behind this dark glass. The lights must run every moment the building is occupied because the useful daylighting zone is only about 16 inches deep. We don't, as we're flipping through the magazines, really recognize the irony in such things.

Designers can learn from building occupants – those who are going to spend two thousand hours a year sitting behind our tinted or clear glass facades. In Terry Gilliam's film Brazil, Robert DeNiro is Harry Tuttle, a Ninja-like building repairman in the future. In this film buildings perform poorly if at all and the bureaucracy that maintains them is indifferent at best. Tuttle's sensible repair skills have been criminalized, and he sneaks around at night, under threat of arrest, to fix buildings. On arrival he whips out an enormous Yankee screwdriver and with swift motions

10.05 a fork in the road

10.06 handheld instruments for measuring buildings-related environmental variables

removes a wall panel. The open wall reveals a complex basal cavity of building guts, which spills into the room. I wonder what that image says about our buildings and their advanced control systems, about our very sophisticated means for producing conditioned interiors.

These observations bring us to a "fork in the road." Many architects are well informed and facile regarding the image and the intentions of architecture but woefully innocent in matters of physical performance. I think the fork in the road is in the context of specialist and specialties. In a compartmentalized design process, where lies the architect? What is the architectural role? Are we to become one of many specialists, secure in our own domain and as incomprehensible to the other specialists as they are to us? Or could we think instead of architects as leaders? As being the one professional charged with seeing the whole of a building, how the different constituent disciplines contribute to it, and how it ends up as a total thing, a whole.

To lead in this way, architects must know more about the physical character of their designs. Our ability to divorce the physical architectural artifact from the means of its conditioning is testimony to the remedial powers of technology, and to the prowess of engineering. Talk to someone that practiced in Arizona in 1940, and show them a proposed glass box many stories tall and a hundred meters long. Ask if this box

should be built in the desert. While possible is such a design reasonable? The designer with experience before 1950 would probably be aware of great costs in the flow of energy and shortfalls in terms of occupant amenity. So ideally would we.

Let me describe the Vital Signs Project, a curriculum materials effort that is being coordinated by the Building Science Group at UC Berkeley. Educators from over two dozen architecture schools have developed instructional materials for the project and fifty other schools have had faculty participate in Vital Signs activities. The project is supported by the Energy Foundation, the National Science Foundation, and the Pacific Gas & Electric Company. We are developing exercises that encourage a greater awareness of energy conservation in architecture, an issue important to sustainability. Rather than isolate energy issues we combine them with an awareness of the physical dimensions of architectural space making, and of occupant well being. The approach is not just about reducing energy, it's also about creating buildings that work for their occupants, and are satisfying to us as designers. The Vital Signs approach has been shaped by a number of previous activities. Many of the educators involved participated in the University of Pennsylvania Passive Solar Curriculum Materials Project. This 1980s project developed instructional materials, and more importantly, brought together faculty from many schools to discuss instruction, to

Charles C. Benton
University of California Berkeley

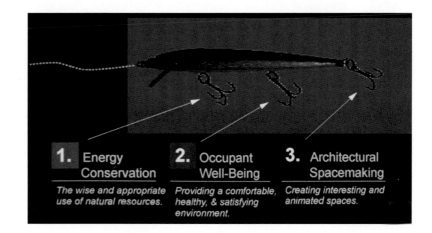

1. Energy Conservation
The wise and appropriate use of natural resources.

2. Occupant Well-Being
Providing a comfortable, healthy, & satisfying environment.

3. Architectural Spacemaking
Creating interesting and animated spaces.

10.07   Issues as Hooks

strategize, and support one another.

I have been long involved in the field investigation of building performance, a continually fascinating experience. For instance, I spent three years in Lockheed Building 157 to see if the daylighting system was effective in admitting natural light to this building. My charge was to see if it did that well and comfortably. It did. I also evaluated the control system to see if it captured savings by reducing electric light. It didn't. For five years the building had only realized about 20% of the possible savings. The problem was commissioning, an issue of equipment tuning. Commissioning is repeatedly problematic in the operation of buildings. In the field one often finds an architectural scheme that makes sense and hardware capable of performing when properly adjusted; but the building didn't work for lack of somebody interested in tuning it.

The Building Science Group at Berkeley has evaluated dozens of buildings from Australia to Michigan for their ability to provide thermal comfort. We examine whether buildings meet the ASHRAE 55-92 Standard and how occupants react to the resulting thermal environments. Our studies are directed toward closing the loop between theory and practice. We've found that buildings by and large meet the standard's physical requirements, but occupants are less satisfied than the standard would assume. We roll a measurement cart up to each sub-

ject's desk to take detailed physical measurements. Feeling that many work environments and having their occupants describe their perceptions has been an invaluable experience. I've come away with the strong sense that people want control over their local workspaces. They want to shape their local environment; to have the amenities of at least a basic Volkswagen: the ability to direct a little heat to their feet, a little breeze to face.

Vital Signs has also been influenced by the Pacific Energy Center (PEC), a remarkable design assistance effort for building professionals run by the Pacific Gas & Electric Company. The PEC is unusual in that it's not targeted to the utility's customers, but rather to those that serve them. The center is for architects, engineers, lighting designers, and facility managers. It has offered over 500 workshops in five years. It provides analysis facilities and loans measurement instruments. One theme emerging from experience at the center is that when architects are thinking about energy conserving features, or trying some new technical approach, they would like to know if the technique has previously worked. They'd like to have the assurance of a case study or some physical awareness as opposed to a simulation. The PEC provides opportunities to examine energy conserving techniques in operation.

The idea of the Vital Signs Project is to ask students to be investigators. We seek to restore an apprecia-

Charles C. Benton
University of California, Berkeley

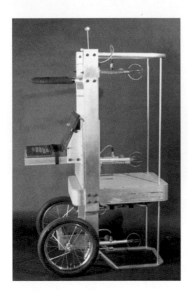

10.08 the Mark II thermal assessement cart from UC Berkeley

tion and understanding of the physical environment within architecture students by encouraging them to develop hypotheses about the performance of existing buildings. What should be happening in this building? Their hypotheses could be derived from images of the buildings, from articles in the literature, from the architects' intentions, or from the building's context. We ask students to visit a building and experience its environment. They talk to the designers and occupants while supplementing their observations with selected measurements. And where appropriate, they report their findings back to the community of architecture schools. We've been using this instructional technique at UC Berkeley, and dozens of other schools, and find it has great potential.

The Vital Signs project is assembling methods for field investigation, and encouraging the promulgation of case studies that are interesting and well done. Our target buildings belong to several categories: historically significant buildings; buildings that shape contemporary architectural thought; buildings designed to conserve energy; and finally, buildings representative of building type. The following are some examples:

Menil Collection Museum, Houston, Texas, Renzo Piano, 1986 – The evocative Menil Gallery sits under a harsh Southern sun with gallery spaces sheltered by a sculptural roof system. What is the light quality like below this trellis-like roof. Does the design serve the conservator as well as the patron? Without visiting we can only imagine how it performs.

Oak Alley Plantation, Vacherie, Louisiana, Juckes Roman, 1839 – A 300-year-old avenue of oaks graces this site. They cast a delightful sea of shade in a hot, muggy landscape. So, the question is what benefit comes from that sea of shade? What is Oak Alley's microclimatic reality? How does it feel to go from sunny field to shadowy refuge? Is it qualitatively different? I can report that it is. What do the numbers look like? Are the temperature differences large?

Logan House, Tampa, Florida, Rowe Holmes Associates, 1982 – These Florida designers decided not to seal the building, but rather to make it as porous as possible. The result is a naturally ventilated house much like Paul Rudolf's early beach houses where the walls were shade and screening. Every Logan House room is ventilated from two or three sides and is designed to use stack effect. The house is raised off the ground to escape the boundary layer, a commonsense and intriguing idea. Fifteen years after construction it would be nice to know if the scheme worked. Does it offer a model to follow or a cautionary tale?

High Museum Addition, Atlanta, Georgia, Richard Meier, 1984 – I lived in Atlanta while they were building Meier's addition to the High Museum of Art. Much

Charles C. Benton
University of California, Berkeley

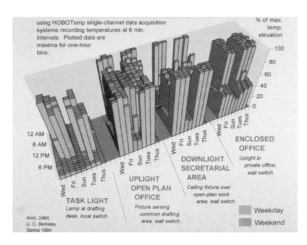

10.09 monitored temperatures reveal distinct lighting patterns in four areasof an architect's office

10.10 the living canopy of Oak Alley's mature oaks

was written – 7 cover articles, 40 or so articles in architectural journals – about this striking building as it opened. The articles uniformly praised Meier's manipulation of daylight. However, on close inspection the building was quite problematic in terms of daylight and the display of art. The pyramidal skylights cited in several articles were covered before the museum even opened in what was to become a major campaign to reduce damaging and excessive light levels. When building had been open only two months they retrofitted the atrium with low-transmittance glass. Later, the museum workshop constructed hundreds of screen-like shading panels and these were placed, sometimes several layers thick, in many of Meier's tidy square windows. The building design simply hasn't worked from lighting and conservation perspectives, important issues in a museum gallery.

Kelbaugh House, Princeton, New Jersey, 1975 – This design provided one of the pervasive images during the '70s discussions of passive solar heating. Trombe walls are one of the 4 major types of passive solar schemes. This example has now operated for 20 years. There were papers in the early years of the house that reported on its operation and performance. Twenty years later we should have a much richer accounting of how this building has performed. How have the people who lived in it responded? Has the scheme evolved?

State of Illinois Center, Chicago, Illinois, Helmut Jahn, 1985 – We know that this glass topped building overheated dramatically. We don't know in great detail about why and how to avoid a similar circumstance. How warm did the building actually get? The remedial course was increasing conditioning capacity to make the upper floors habitable. How much did they add? With the added cooling how has it turned out?

United Airlines Terminal, Chicago, Illinois, Helmut Jahn, 1984 – This is an engaging space for the traveler and one of the early applications of fritted glass, seen as a solution to solar gain. Fritted glass is a handsome material, but when writ large as in the United Airlines Terminal, does it provide sufficient solar control? The terminal now has retrofit interior shading screens. What is their story?

Douglas House, Harbor Springs, Michigan, Richard Meier, 1973 – One immutable lesson during my education was that architecture, if great enough, can suspend physics. A case in point is Richard Meier's Douglas House with its four-story-high, west-facing, single-glazed, clear-glass façade facing Lake Michigan. Lacking operable windows, exterior shading, and interior shading on the west façade causes one to imagine the house to be near uninhabitable on a summer afternoon. I would dearly like to know how the house performs. It would be interesting to document its occupancy periods. The more I have

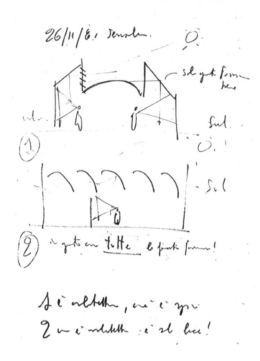

10.11 the "soft pencil" - an early Renzo Piano sketch for the Menil Collection Museum

thought about the house, the more I've developed an appreciation for the Douglas' dedication as architectural patrons.

Rock & Roll Hall of Fame, Cleveland, Ohio, I. M. Pei, 1995 – This building was originally designed with its sloping glass atrium facing north, and then a late project site change flipped the glass roof around to face south. The adjustment was in the tonnage of cooling equipment as opposed to the architectural fabric.

Gregory Bateson Building, Sacramento, California, Sim Van der Ryn, 1979 – In the mid '80s there was a flurry of publicity about the State of California state office buildings, designed while Sim van Der Ryn was the state architect. The program produced a half-dozen office buildings designed to conserve energy. As these buildings approach 20 years of operation how well are the performing? It would be interesting to know if they are successful as low energy buildings. Are they models we should follow?

San Francisco Public Library, San Francisco, California, SMWM, 1995 – This design attended to indoor air quality issues with great vigor. In material selection and the design process measures were taken to safeguard interior air quality. It would be a fine study to examine the cross talk between indoor air quality strategies and other issues such as acoustics.

Each of these buildings has stories to tell and valuable lessons for students and practitioners alike. Information from studies of their post-occupancy performance could inform student design sensibilities. Furthermore, if students routinely assessed buildings they would have direct experience with engineering values – with the lux, degrees, amps, and meters/second that emerge from calculations and standards. They would know how 20 degrees feels verses 30 degrees and why humidity plays a role in higher ambient temperatures. They would understand the difference between 100 lux, 1,000 lux and 10,000 lux. If students investigated buildings they would also compare the intent of the designer to the outcome of the building, and appreciate mediating factors like the construction process, operational decisions, and intervention by the occupants. These factors come into play in fascinating ways. With such experience students could, and should, gauge the efficacy of standards that guide design (e.g., the ASHRAE 55-92 Thermal Comfort standard, the IES recommended practices for lighting.)

To date, the Vital Signs Project has mounted several initiatives in support of instruction. We have developed, reviewed, and distributed a set of instructional Resource Packages on topics ranging from glazing to thermal mass to solar control devices. Each package includes an exposition covering the principles of that package's topic, a bibliography, and a guide to standard practices. It then provides a set of

Charles C. Benton
University of California, Berkeley

field protocols for the evaluation of buildings. What could one learn from a building during a single day? What could one learn from a few visits and handheld instrumentation? What could one learn from continued monitoring? In concert with the American Collegiate Schools of Architecture (ACSA), Vital Signs has conducted a series of five-day summer training sessions for educators interested in the approach. We have also conducted two rounds of teaching incentive grants awarded on the basis of peer-reviewed proposals and two rounds of a juried competition for student-conducted case studies.

Finally, we have put together an instrument loan program providing sets of measurement devices to 10 schools per year. This allows educators to experiment with the Vital Signs approach. Instrumentation is quite different now as compared to 20 years ago. We have a fascinating array of devices that can be brought to bear in helping us understand the physical performance patterns of a realized design. Let me show two examples. The first is a single channel temperature logger. You plug this device into a microcomputer, you say "collect temperature data every five minutes". It'll do that for several weeks. You could place such a device under a table, or in the podium, and return weeks later to harvest a record of the temperature in that location. If you place the data logger in a light fixture you could determine when the fixture was on, and when it was

off. If you connect it to a small $20 occupancy sensor, you can tell when this room was occupied, and when it was not. The second device, a small handheld pyrameter, can point to surfaces and measure their temperature remotely – the ceiling is 63 degrees. If you went into a naturally ventilated building curious about the stack effect, you could measure up and down the stack, and examine the surface temperatures that drive its airflow.

The Vital Signs Project aims to return issues of physical performance to the architectural domain. A work in progress, our experience to date has been quite positive. Educators are adopting the approach in their courses. Participation in the Vital Signs summer training sessions, student competitions, faculty teaching grant, and toolkit loan programs has kept these programs at capacity for five years. We are distributing project artifacts, including case studies, in printed form and via the Internet. The electronic dissemination delivers Vital Signs materials to audiences beyond the primary target (North American architecture programs) without incremental cost. Our ultimate objective is to inform the sensibilities of the designer, to feed experiences gained by listening to buildings back into the soft pencil sketch. And to have that sketch represent a building that is environmentally responsible, experientially engaging, and architecturally satisfying.

Vivian Loftness
Carnegie Mellon University

11.00 section through the Intelligent Workplace, Carnegie Mellon
University

Addressing the Big Building Crisis in Sustainability: Communities, Infrastructures, and Indoor Environments

Vivian Loftness
Carnegie Mellon University
Pittsburgh, Pennsylvania, U.S.A.

11.01 shading to the external wall of the Intelligent Workplace, Center for Building Performance and Diagnostics, Carnegie Mellon University.

I and the group in the Center for Building Diagnostics and Performance at Carnegie Mellon have been actively involved with evaluating existing buildings. The more time you spend in existing buildings the more urgent environmental design becomes. I want to focus upon what is happening in both the public and corporate sectors. The General Service Administration has been in the process of trying to distribute America's workers out of downtown D.C., or central D.C. because there was a tremendous mandate on increasing roadway, and it was costing America too much to keep widening the roads. So they were trying to set up satellite telecommuting offices out in those areas where thousands of workers lived, to get them to stay at least one or two days a week in their own communities. This would mean that that they actually could go to the Little League after school, and they could see the kids play, and they could be part of their family, and not have to get up at 4:00 in the morning. The problem was how they were going to go about doing that. They were basically going to put out a joint 'request fro proposals', and every developer in America was going to run around, trying to build this stuff for satellite offices in rural Virginia and rural Maryland. I want to address an issue about urban development. Even if we're dealing, in some cases, with suburban sites we're still addressing mixed use pedestrian environments; we're still addressing the issue of life where you're not constantly spending large chunks of time on the road. These scars on

the landscape are one of the things we're trying to change. The other scar on the landscape that we're trying to change is the American propensity for the massive floor plate. The bigger the building, the more economical it seems to be for the developer who is making a large profit on a long term gain. And you can build them something very cheap and make a lot of money on the basis of a 20 year lease from the Federal Government.

The Construction Engineering Research Laboratory in Champaign, Illinois has a campus that is a series of lab buildings. Laboratory work has changed over time. They found out that what they really need is electronic labs which happen to be offices. And of course you can imagine the developers of Champaign immediately coming in with the perfect solution; least cost. "We can give you electronic labs — quasi offices — in this form." Or another developer coming in very quickly and saying "I can do warehouse offices. We have no fire escapes, we have no egress problems. Look at how much we can save. And I can give you buildings like this." These are non-sustainable solutions. There is nothing there. There's no purpose to go to visit them. Obviously you go there to work because that's where your job and your livelihood is. And the question is; can we not afford to build fabric? Fabric that leads to future fabric. Fabric that leads to mixed use, and leads to continuity in already devastated sites. And the answer is; yes we can, but we have to realign our

Effective Design of Facilities to Support Productivity

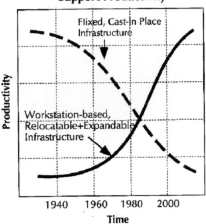

11.02 new buildings that are designed with inflexible infrastructures will continue to be incapable of supporting the electronic age in office productivity.

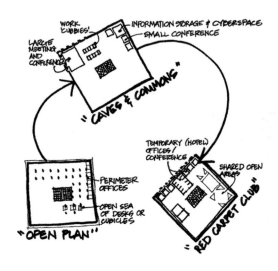

11.03 alternatives to the vast open plan: dynamic tasks and organizations will need the ability to continuously reconfigure workplace types over time and space.

resources. Maybe they don't go into another interchange or clover leaf road intersection, but go into the actual built environment and the physical infrastructure.

In a proposal for the company, Searle in Champaign Illinois, we sought to start that process. Their first new electronic office building that they built is a lab-like building that is much too deep for daylight, and access to the natural environment. And we basically said "No, let's go back to skin-dominated buildings and solve the environmental forces in the most positive fashion." The big building propensity, which is rampant in the United States where there is no law that guarantees access to a window for any worker in America, is now being exported. And we are exporting those big buildings in lots of shapes, typically tall ones arising from a fascination with America and what America represents. Most of those buildings have massive floor plates. Not thin buildings, massive floor plates that in turn mean that workers have no access to daylight. All the electric fixtures have to be on.

We look at the environment as really a negative factor, and of course the devastation on the ground plane for these kinds of buildings is also serious. There are, in many cases 40,000 workers stacked vertically. That is a town. And they have to go in and out of typically a single point of entry every day. Typically at two time periods. So we're creating this

sort of massive infrastructural system with money that has to be spent but could in fact be built in a very, very different way. There is a massive amount of introduction of new technology, and as Bill Mitchell alluded to, what is this technology going to mean?. Wireless technology, microtechnology, and remote technology. We're working very hard on trying to anticipate what it does mean, and whether architecture is going to get better or worse. We're at the fork in the road. Architecture can either get better with technology, or it can get much, much worse.

Here are the things that organizations in America are talking about that, technology is doing for them. They say "We're going to go flatter, less hierarchial organizational structures. We're going to have more teamwork. We're going to have smaller teams. We're going to have multidisciplinary teams. We're going to have multiple work stations. We're going to have telecommuting. Yes, we're going to have quality of life improvement. We're going to have diversity of job descriptions. We're going to have massive changes in density of workers. Some organizations are going to have only a few workers, some are going to have lots of high density. Call centers, everybody standing one by the other and answering phones and taking your CD orders. Diversity and density of space required and service required. We'll have more desktop, we'll have miniaturization. We'll have non-hierarchical control of air temperature and light — at least those are my dreams.

		Number of storeys	Typical floor size	Typical office depth	Furthest distance from perimeter aspect	Efficiency: net to gross	Maximum cellularisation % of usable	Type of core	Type of HVAC service
▬	Traditional North American Speculative office	80	3000 m²	18 m	18 m	90%	20%	Concentrated	Centralized
ᴫᴫᴫ	The new North European office	5	200 m²	10 m	5 m	70% (lots of public circulation)	80%	Dispersed	Decentralized: minimal use of HVAC

(*The Intelligent Building in Europe,* DEGW, 1992)

11.04 European buildings generally give workers a far better access to windows : from The Intelligent Building in Europe by DEGW.

Certainly we'll have increased computing capacity, and with that increased power demands, and eventually a merging of data, voice, and video. And the hardware for this stuff — which used to be the old Remington or whatever version of typewriter you started on — through the PC, to all the networked PCs, to what we're looking at on desktops today, and things that are in people's pockets and briefcases. And architecture is either going to respond or not respond. It's either going to respond in a sustainable fashion, or it's going to respond in whatever is expedient, and will make a big profit. With this technology shift, the companies are going through significant indoor space planning strategies. They're starting from open plan and saying "Well that's not quite working. Let's go to something called caves and commons, or personal harbors and coves." There are many terms for looking at small spaces that you can call home, and then more teaming spaces. They're looking at red carpet clubs similar to what you see at the airport where you have no territorial base at all. You don't have a desk. You just come in, and pick a space that's wonderful. And as they bandy these things around, in most cases they are talking about strategies inside massive building floor plates; and it just doesn't work. It's a mess.

When we go and do field evaluations of buildings. An example of one of those floor plates is an office building, about 200 by 200 feet on two floors. There are nine people in that place that have a window. So what are we seeing? We're seeing stresses that are repetitive again and again. The users are good sensors but you can go in and monitor it with diagnostic equipment as well. We've got cooling problems, we've got ventilation problems, we've actually got lighting problems because of the high light levels in some cases, and low in other cases. We've got clear access to windows issues, and territoriality and rank problems, which is a qualitative issue. We have voice connectivity, data connectivity, and power connectivity. We've got wall system and special modification problems. We've got ceiling system and closure problems with acoustics, and we've got work storage and access problems which are pervasive. Now why do we have these problems? Because underneath these massive floor plates is the cheapest, stripped down system that we could get away with by code. And I do like the expression that explains codes as the minimum you can do by law. That's it; that's the worst case you can do, and still be within the legal limit. It's not quality design.

We have HVAC, heating, ventilation, air conditioning system controls in buildings, and in some cases on a floor of several hundred people there'll be four thermostats controlling four zones. It's obviously driven by environmental forces on four sides of the building, and then the core is all lumped together. What if you had dynamic space planning, and dynamic equipment loading? Which of course we do. How are we going to cope with that when we've only got four

11.05 "least- cost officing": the trend to move workforces into warehouse offices, with minimum individual environmental quality

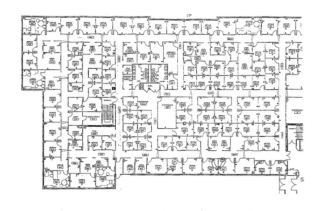

11.06 the anonymous deep plan: within the tradition of poor indoor environmental quality, some employers justify moving offices into empty warhouses or strip malls, or newly built least-cost solutions.

thermostats, and one corner of the building has been laid out as a red carpet club with lots of people, another corner is laid out as an executive suite with a few people, and some people have lots of equipment, and some do not.

Almost every international building that we've studied that has been trying to call itself an advanced building, building for sustainability, building for long life, has increased zoning in many cases and in the best cases down to a zone per work station. Every person you put in that building has a dedicated right to thermal control. Now obviously that's the best case, and many buildings feel they can't cost-justify that, and they back off. The Omeda Center in Japan has 25 zones per floor. That means four to six people are negotiating the thermostat. Maybe that's OK except if those four to six people have very, very different thermal demands. In which case you'd be back in trouble.

Lighting control is getting better because the technology is getting cheaper. But for a while we had a single switch. The whole floor had to be lit up in order for anybody to get light. We're now getting down to zones of light where you may have a switch that services 20 people. Obviously the ideal situation is you have a switch for every person in the building. Networking is the same. Buildings have been trying to sneak away with the cheapest solution which is a "poke through" which basically means that you go to

the office below. You punch a hole through the ceiling and put a box above it which has data, power, voice capability; and people of course fall over them, or roll their chairs into them. In the World Trade Center I am told that if you want to add an additional data, power, voice outlet box you have to fill four holes because the structural integrity of the slab is in question. Now we have been doing this because it is cheap in first costs. It is extremely expensive in long term costs. And of course it's very disruptive because the people down below are constantly being bothered if you want to change your box. In a lot of cases you don't move the box, you just live with the fact that every time you get up off your chair you fall.

The second best thing that was tried was a trench system as, for example, with the high tech office for Packard Bell in Northern California. They basically said "No you can't keep changing the boxes. We're a computer-intensive company." Casting it in concrete and setting it up typically somewhere in the order of 30 access ports for 300 people. That means 10 people are sharing an access port. There are lots of little power strips, and little redundant daisy chains that help all these people plug in because it's undersized for real density of occupants in buildings. And they mix that with a cellular deck, which is the next slightly more expensive, with a fixed grid of access ports. In this case we're told that Pack Bell charges the users $1,000 for every new data port that has to be put into a desk because it is so full of

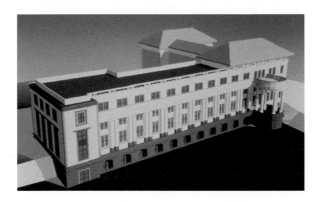

11.07 the rooftop location for the new Intelligent Workplace at Carnegie Mellon University.

11.08 computer model of the Intelligent Workplace.

wire that they are at the point they cannot pull stuff any more. They have to find alternative routes. That kind of expense could easily be rolled back into first cost.

Here is a typical problem that a CEO of an organization wants to double the density of his workers in his office building; this is happening all over the country right now. Actually the CFO, the Chief Financial Officer, sends by fax a message to all the facility managers in his buildings "From this day forward we will reduce from 160 square foot per worker to 80 square foot per worker. Thank you very much. Signed, CFO." He has absolutely no idea of the implications of that. And of course the facilities guys around the country are desperately trying to downsize. They're rushing to every furniture manufacturer in the world and saying "I need to go to eight by eight modules now. Can you do that for me?" And they say "Yes, we can do that for you." Well of course the infrastructure underneath has nothing to do with getting air to every desk, getting light to every desk, getting networks to every desk. So we have to start with this as a sustainable minimum: every worker in the building deserves fresh air. That means outside air taken to the desk. Every worker deserves temperature control. Every worker deserves lighting control. Every worker deserves daylight and view. A little hard in the giant buildings and complexes of America right now. Every worker deserves a certain level of privacy and working quiet

— not easy to achieve. Everyone deserves network access which means multiple data, multiple power, and multiple voice connections. They also deserve ergonomic furniture, and environmentally appropriate finishes. So if we take that as given, we're going to have a different set of solutions both in new buildings and in existing buildings.

This is what we give workers in the United States by law. We give them a variable air supply totally dependent on thermal demand. So if you don't have a thermal demand you get no air. We give them a blanket supply of cooling with large zones of fifteen people average. We give them uniform high level lighting, which we don't need for computer work, and the uniformity has other kinds of problems. We rarely give them daylight and view — a complete isolation from the outdoors —and rarely working quiet or privacy because those are not affordable as such. We give them one data connection, two power, one voice. This is a typical office. And we give them pre-computer furniture; non-ergonomic, with unmeasured indoor pollutant sources. This is the sort of standard practice that's out there.

What are we suggesting? We're suggesting a move: a dramatic, complete, and from this day forward move away from blanket and idiosyncratic solutions into nodal, user-based infrastructures. So basically, rather than sort of washing the whole building with air, and light, and a few idiosyncratic zones for the

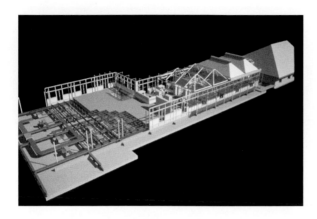

11.09 the building system as constructed above on the roof of Margaret Morrison Carnegie Hall.

11.10 completed elevation with solar shading and new rooftop lighting, Center for Building Performance and Diagnostics, Carnegie Mellon University.

board and the boardroom where you give them individual thermostats, and individual dimming switches on their lights, you go to a system where you establish a grid. The grid provides an infrastructure of service, and the nodes can be relocated by the end user. If you want to increase the density of users you have to make sure that the grid can support it. When you get in an elevator, there's a label on the elevator door that says "This elevator can hold ten people or X number of pounds." But whenyou step out of the elevator there's no label that says "This floor can support 100 people. That's all the air that's been designed into the ducts and the air handling unit. That's all the chilling capacity that's in here. That's all the power capacity that's in here." There's no label. And so the CFO can send a message down, and we can double the density, and find ourselves in real deep environmental trouble. We call this a flexible grid, flexible density, flexible closure technologies or systems. They're a constellation of building systems that permit each individual or work station to set the location and density of heating, cooling, ventilation, lighting, telecommunications and furniture including the level of work space and closure.

The last infrastructure that we have got to provide for workers is access to windows. I cannot emphasize this more. In new construction, we should basically rise up together and say "No more massive footprints." Not in the United States, not anywhere in the world, because they are non-sustainable. It is of course trivial if you establish a code requirement that every worker has a seated view of a window. It just goes away. We have managed to pass in this country a law that guarantees access for everybody in a wheelchair to every building; but we cannot pass a law that guarantees access for the workers to windows. And the cost implications are possibly parallel. There are cost implications, but it's certain that as a humanitarian gesture, it has a long term impact on productivity and health in the workplace, and a direct relationship to the unproductivity of sick building syndrome.

Vivian Loftness
Carnegie Mellon University

Ellen Dunham-Jones
Massachusetts Institute of Technology

12.00 parking garage in sprawl environment. Fairfax, Virginia, 1997

Massachusetts Institute of Technology

Comment: Questioning the Stand-Alone Building

Ellen Dunham-Jones
Massachusetts Institute of Technology
Cambridge, Massachusetts, U.S.A.

12.01 strip development. Manassas, Virginia, 1989

The profession of architecture has defined "the dimensions of sustainability" from a variety of perspectives. In the 1970s, solar cabins in the woods were associated with the counter-culture and alternative lifestyles. In the '90s, parallel but uncoordinated efforts at sustainability have developed between approaches more aligned with urban design or with engineering. In the former, dimensionality is associated with the kind of broadening of perspective brought on by a systemic environmental approach. Architecture's sustainability is judged in relation to its role in urban and regional systems. The latter approach works at the scale of the individual building and its precisely detailed components designed to minimize energy use or maximize energy production. In this case, the dimensions of interest are the quantifiable measures of the building's self-sufficiency. Ideal performance is represented by the "stand-alone" building. Able to produce its own power and recycle its own waste, the stand-alone building seemingly does not contribute to environmental degradation. However, the engineered ideal of a self-sufficient building is too often at odds with the urban design ideal of a self-sufficient town or region. As a step towards allowing these two approaches to better complement each other and without demeaning the stand-alone building's obvious benefits, I want to point out its limitations from a social and urban design perspective.

The engineering-oriented fascination with performance criteria serves a useful purpose in convincing clients of the economic value of energy-conserving measures. Daylighting can be correlated to employee productivity. Natural ventilation can be indexed to employee health. Operating costs can be compared with construction costs for various energy-reducing or energy-producing systems. Outside governmental regulation, such calculations are perhaps the most effective means of advancing the collective cause of sustainability because they reveal how environmentally friendly measures serve the individual client's self-interest. However, the translation of collective benefits into individual benefits is far from direct when screened through cost analysis. While an ecologically based understanding of environment emphasizes inter-relationships and systemic networks, performance-based comparisons tend to examine each project as an isolated phenomena of calculated inputs and outputs. That which cannot easily be measured, or which is not an immediate cost to the client, tends to be left out of the equation. The energy costs associated with global warming, non-renewable resources, embodied energy, and transportation have a global impact but only an indirect affect on the performance of the building from a client's perspective, and as such are relatively absent from performance-oriented analyses. Instead, (and without a trace of irony) such analyses

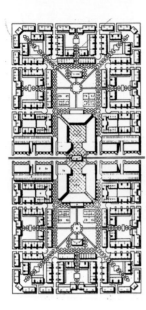

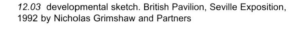

12.02 generic diagram for 60 acre Pedestrian Pocket by Peter Calthorpe

12.03 developmental sketch. British Pavilion, Seville Exposition, 1992 by Nicholas Grimshaw and Partners

present sustainability in terms of the single object.

This has been most emphatic in the glorification of the stand-alone building. Whether a low-impact eco-resort or a daylit manufacturing facility, stand-alone buildings have been presented to us as ideals of self-sufficiency. Able to produce as much, if not more, energy than they consume, their independence from utility companies allows them to locate wherever they like, to literally stand alone. Unfortunately, this is also where the problem lies. Buildings that stand alone also stand apart — from the city, people, and transport.

Most of the contemporary buildings held up as models of self-sufficiency have to be driven to. Stand-alone buildings tend to locate in either exotic, remote sites and or on low-density exurban fringes where they can control access to sunlight, wind and soil. Unfortunately, such strategies tend to preclude urban infill sites and instead encourage sprawl and decentralization. While they may stand alone from collective power and waste systems, they are very much engaged with transportation networks, exacerbating problems of impervious road surfacing, erosion, the delimiting and contamination of wild animal habitats, depletion of fossil fuels, and pollution from cars and trucks. Such transportation costs rarely figure into the client's costs or the performance criteria cited for

stand-alone buildings. Less prominent, they nonetheless add significantly to the problems of unsustainability. In fact, due in large part to decentralized development's mandated use of the automobile, transportation accounts for approximately one third of all energy use in the U.S. (1).

Hal Harvey, executive director of The Energy Foundation, argues that there are principally two ways to reduce transportation energy use (2).The first is the technofix: improve the fuel efficiency of the car, play with alternative fuels, various Intelligent Highway Vehicle Systems (IHVS), etc. The technofix has made great strides since the oil crises of the '70s. Unfortunately however, the effect of the gains in efficiency and emissions control have been largely neutralized by the greater numbers of vehicles on the road and the accompanying growth in average vehicle miles travelled per year — now climbing at twice the rate of population growth (3). Christopher Flavin and Nicholas Lenssen of the Worldwatch Institute write:

> No matter how much less polluting
> automobiles become in the future,
> one thing is clear: they will not be
> a panacea for the world's trans-
> portation problems. Although the
> new technologies could greatly
> reduce many of the energy related

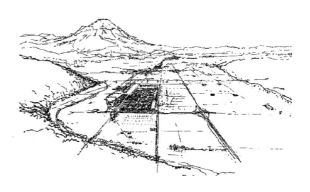

12.04 proposal for Green River Valley, outside Seattle, by Peter Calthorpe and Doug Kelbaugh

problems caused by cars, they could exacerbate others, including the suburban sprawl, congestion, and destruction of neighborhoods that is rampant in so many parts of the world. This suggests that the redesign of the automobile must be accompanied by efforts to spur an array of new transportation options and to change regional development patterns so as to reduce the need for travel and create more livable communities (4).

Flavin and Lenssen suggest that in addition to the technofix, we need an urban design fix.

I would argue that the same applies to architecture. The stand-alone building is a technofix. Like electric vehicle or IHVS systems, it relies on technical solutions, passive or active, mostly to do with making a more energy efficient building envelope. However, without more attention to an urban design fix, the worthwhile gains are likely to be offset by inefficient lower density land-use patterns.

One need only look at the tremendous growth in sprawl and land consumption since the 1970s to appreciate the environmental dangers of making it

technologically easier for people to move further away from city centers and their services (5). Christopher Leinberger, a noted real estate analyst, points out that between 1970 and 1990, Chicago's population grew 4% while its size grew 45%. This is due to the growth in the exurban rings that now extend some sixty miles beyond the downtown. Los Angeles is even more extreme. In the same time period its population grew 45% while its size grew 300% (6)! At least five and a half square miles of rural land are converted each day in the U.S. to urban, suburban, or other uses (7). Not surprisingly, the spreading of the low-density landscape has been accompanied by a doubling of the vehicle miles travelled per capita in the U.S. since 1960 (8). The distance between buildings makes them extremely difficult to serve efficiently with public transport, such that commuting by private car is all but required by decentralized development.

Even telecommuting, a dream solution raised by those looking for more technofixes, still promotes further decentralization and sprawl. By allowing the place of work to be detached from proximity to other people and uses, telecommuting cuts down on work trips, but not the, now lengthened, non-work trips (9). Despite significant advances in various forms of telecommunications and modest increases in the number of "electronic cottages" operating from

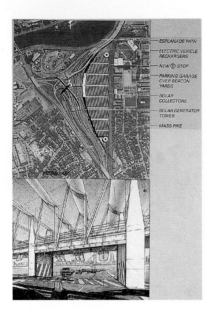

12.05 electric vehicle tollbooths delivering surplus energy to the local utility. Redesigned Massachusetts Turnpike. by Ellen Dunham-Jones, 1995

12.06 redesigned tollbooths integrate the techno-fix into an urban design fix. by Ellen Dunham-Jones, 1995

remote mountain tops or beachfronts, car use has only increased. From 1970 to 1990, the percentage of U.S. households with three or more cars jumped from 7% to 18% (10).

Concern over the environmental consequences of sprawl and the increased reliance on private automobiles has prompted a number of architects to develop sustainable urban design strategies. The environmental virtues of compact, transport-oriented, mixed-use and mixed-income developments — whether in the form of urban infill, suburban retrofit, or greenfield projects — have recently been extolled by a variety of professionals interested in reducing and slowing car trips, promoting communal engagement through pedestrianized public places, protecting regional habitats and generally resisting sprawl (11). Sadly, the profession of architecture is currently sharply, but unnecessarily, divided between these environmentalist efforts by "new urbanists" to join regional- and master-planning and the environmentalist work of "high-tech" architects manipulating the forms of individual buildings so as to exploit wind and solar power, natural ventilation, daylighting, etc. To date, there has been far too little conversation between the neo-traditional architecture and urbanism of the former group (with the resistance many of its members have to modernist styles) and the high-tech object-focused work of the latter (and their gen-

eral disdain for traditional architectural styles and urban patterns). Unfortunately, though interest in energy efficient building envelopes and energy efficient urban design are hardly mutually exclusive, stylistic differences have clouded the contributions each could make to the other. This professional gap has to be closed before architects can seriously employ the full range of tactics necessary to significantly advance us towards a more sustainable environment. Happily, the gap is unnecessary and I, for one, am optimistic that the power of the concept of sustainability will invoke greater architectural integration of innovative engineering with more compact planning strategies.

It will also be necessary for architects to consider the social dimensions of sustainability. The withdrawal of stand-alone buildings from public spaces and services into private domains has unintentional overtones of survivalists or militias who forsake participatory democracy for self-sufficiency and controlled enclaves. Robert Reich, former Secretary of Labor under President Clinton, has described the increasing secession of the wealthy from the poor into gated communities and fortified enclaves in similar terms (12). Both groups abandon communal responsibilities to anyone but themselves. Aided and abetted by new technologies and decentralized development, this social and spatial segregation is on the rise and

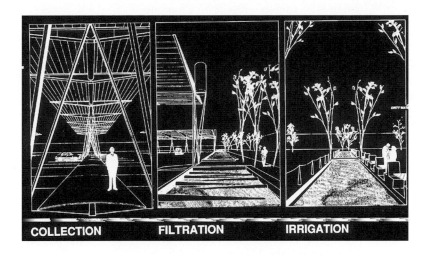

Ellen Dunham-Jones
Massachusetts Institute of Technology

COLLECTION FILTRATION IRRIGATION

12.07 retrofitting the parking lot. Park / Park competition: Public Space in the New American City. 1994. by Dunham-Jones and LeBlanc Architects with Reiter and Reiter Architects.

mirrors the widening income gap between rich and poor (13). The immobile urban poor are distanced from the new jobs on the exurban, privatized periphery and left to fend for themselves in a city with degraded public services and infrastructure. This is in contrast to traditional urban structures where self-sufficiency outside the city was understood as a deprived condition relative to the superior services offered by the city. Its infrastructure for defense, water supply, power, etc., provided cities with monumental walls, bridges, wells, and damns that defined the city as a collective enterprise dedicated to providing the good life for its citizens. Today, "public" is often associated with "shabby" and second-rate. Instead of living well together, contemporary development patterns reveal the degree to which communal ties are increasingly frayed. The city as a place of shared destiny and inter-relationships has been increasingly replaced by individual self-sufficiency. Stand-alone buildings contribute to this formation of removed, individualistic, privatized domains. Something of a contradiction in terms, they make sustainability exclusive.

It is because I have such tremendous respect for the work involved with self-sufficiency that I offer these criticisms. I greatly admire designs that have proved themselves capable of standing alone, working within the limits of available conditions such that they

neither pollute nor consume natural resources. My hopes for such a model compel me to want to further coordinate the work done at this scale with that being done at the larger urban and regional scale. Even if we can produce buildings that are internally energy efficient, given population predictions for 2050 of half again as many people in the U.S. and double the worldwide population, we simply cannot afford more sprawl. Nor can we afford to continue to socially and economically segregate our society. By better integrating building and urban design, the profession of architecture can truly contribute to a society that is sustainable economically, socially, and environmentally.

Ellen Dunham-Jones
Massachusetts Institute of Technology

1. In addition, transportation is also responsible for nearly 30% of total U.S. carbon emissions. Cars and trucks alone consume 63% of all petroleum in the country. *The Energy Foundation, 1995* (San Francisco, CA: The Energy Foundation, p. 24).

2. Hal Harvey, presentation to the Congress For The New Urbanism III, San Francisco CA, February 18, 1995.

3. *The Energy Foundation, 1995, ibid.* Since 1990 alone, American driving is estimated to have increased 18%. *A Blueprint for ISTEA Reauthorization* (Washington DC: Surface Transportation Policy Project, 1997, p.6.)

4. Production of automobiles has gone from roughly 50 million worldwide in 1950 to approx. 600 million in 1994. Christopher Flavin and Nicholas Lenssen, *Power Surge, Guide to the Coming Energy Revolution*, Worldwatch Environmental Alert Series, (W.W. Norton & Company, NY, 1994 p. 198).

5. Advanced telecommunications have allowed the back offices of the service economy to migrate out of downtown locations, fuelling exurban sprawl. See, Ellen Dunham-Jones, "Temporary Contracts; The Economy of the Post-Industrial Landscape", *Harvard Design Magazine*, Fall 1997.

6. Christopher B. Leinberger, presentation to the Congress For The New Urbanism III, San Francisco, CA, February 18, 1995.

7. V. Gail Easley, "Staying Inside the Lines: Urban Growth Boundaries", *Planning Advisory Service Report no. 440*, American Planning Association, Chicago, 1992.

8. Interpolated from figure 4, a graph presented by Hal Harvey in "Essay From the Executive Director", *The Energy Foundation, 1994* (San Francisco, CA: The Energy Foundation, p. 4).

9. This issue is further complicated by comparing trip lengths. Telecommuting from home enables greater sprawl. However, telecommuting centers outside the home can reintroduce a centralizing focus to development and reduce commute distances. Small neighborhood telecommuting centers in Chula Vista, California double as classrooms at night, and are estimated to save 5000 miles of driving each month. See Environmental Protection Agency, brochure EPA 230-F-96-003, *Smart Moves*, August 1996.

10. Surface Transportation Policy Project, *ibid.* Thomas C. Palmer Jr. reported in *The Boston Globe* that nationally, the number of homes with three-car garages has grown steadily from 11% of new single-family homes in 1992 — the first year multiple garages were tabulated by the US Census Bureau — to 13% in 1994. "Tripling the Premium on Parking Spaces", March 20, 1995, p.13-17.

11. These proposals have coalesced within an inter-disciplinary movement called new urbanism. For a discussion of the environmental agenda within new urbanism see Doug Kelbaugh, *Common Place, Toward Neighborhood and Regional Design* (Seattle: University of Washington Press, 1997) and Peter Calthorpe, *The Next American Metropolis, Ecology, Community and the American Dream* (New York: Princeton Architectural Press, 1993).

12. Robert Reich, *The Work of Nations, Preparing Ourselves for 21st - Century Capitalism* (New York, Random House, Vintage Books, 1992).

13. The Human Development Report of the United Nations Development Programme cites a dramatic enlargement of global income differences in the past three decades. In 1960 the wealthiest 20% of the world population had more than thirty times the income of the poorest 20%. In 1989 that figure had grown to more than sixty times, such that the richest 20% of the population held 82.7% of global income. This comparison relates to the distribution between rich and poor countries. If one also looks at the income disparities within countries, the richest 20% of the world population have at least 150 times the income of the poorest 20%. Ingomar Hauchler and Paul M. Kennedy eds., *Global Trends, The World Almanac of Development and Peace* (New York: Continuum, 1994, p.54). Within the United States, Robert Reich writes, "For most of the nation's history, poorer towns and regions steadily gained ground on wealthier areas, as American industry spread to Southern and Western states in search of cheap labor. This trend ended sometime in the 1970s, as American industry moved on to Mexico, Southeast Asia, and other places around the world... American cities and counties with the lowest per-person incomes in 1979 had dropped even further below the nation's average by the late 1980s; cities and counties with the highest incomes headed in the opposite direction." *ibid.* p.272.

Ellen Dunham-Jones
Massachusetts Institute of Technology

13.00 glass roof detail suspended from masts: The International School in Lyon

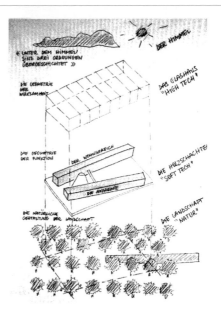

The Micro Climate Envelope

Gilles Perraudin
Jourda & Perraudin, Architects
Lyon, France

13.01 diagram of the concept for the microclimatic layers: Training Center in Herne-Sodingen, Germany

For the past 15 years our office has produced a great number of projects; approximately 200. Most of them are lost competition projects, and they have not had a chance to be built, of course. Some of them are now realized in their construction. It is possible to explain and describe projects in different ways; technical, economic, brief, program, and so on. But I have chosen to discuss a small selection of projects and buildings considering the relation between architecture and its natural environment as an attempt to design an architecture conscious of the fragility of the conditions of our life on the Earth. Each project develops its own concept, related to its specific brief. But all of them could be gathered into a main idea which could be called the concept of a "microclimatic envelope".

This concept, an overall secondary envelope, sheltering in our buildings results from an idea developed for the design of an education center for the Minister of the Interior for North Rhine Westphalie region in Germany. The project, which was the winning entry in the architectural competition in 1992, was designed according to this theory. It responded to a number of preoccupations relative to the protection of the environment. Reduction of energy consumption, use of ecological materials, recycling rainwater, decontamination of the soil, and so on. Decontamination because we are in a rural region, and there's a lot of old coal mines in this region. And not all the soil, but most of the parts of the region are

contaminated. Apart from just the energy performance of this envelope, we proposed another way of using space, an alternative relationship between buildings and their environment, between the user and their surroundings. The limit between inside and outside no longer exists as a rigid boundary. It changes according to climatic conditions. The concept of a microclimatic envelope tends to bring together under the auspices of one team a number of architectural theories explored in previous projects and buildings. In order to expose what is encompassed by this concept, which is no more than a step in the direction of an environmentally conscious architecture, it is necessary to evoke these architectural theories developed in different past projects.

We have worked on this subject since the creation of our office in 1980. These principles are the house within the house, or the Rochandal principle, transitional spaces, the double facade, the overall cover or shelter structure, the total space. The image conjured up by Rochandal illustrates a particular special disposition: a successive encasement of volumes, thus giving a hierarchical layering of living areas from the interior, very protected spaces, to the exterior spaces. This theory of Rochandal is fully developed in the project for an individual house for the first European competition for passive solar energy. We won this ideas competition in 1980. The project systematically organizes progressive enclosing of living spaces, as well as the use of

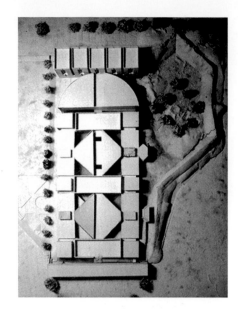

13.02 model of the solar house exemplifying the Rochandal principle: the house extends out in accordance with the climate.

13.03 study model for La Lanterne school in Cergy-Pontoise

different materials for each of these successive houses. Therefore, each envelope around the central core of the house develops a different architecture according to the climatic requirements of each space. Thus we find in succession the central core of a house, a minimal area of 40 square meters housing the essential living space. This is built from in situ concrete, giving a high thermal mass, and grouping all the heat sources within the home: kitchen, chimney, bathroom, and so on. Then comes the house proper of 120 square meters composed of traditional living spaces: large bedroom, living room, play room, built in concrete block work. Each area of this second living space constitutes an extension of the central core. The bedrooms form an extension of a bed alcove of the inner house.

The third house is a non-insulated timber structure offering diverse living area during the mid-seasons. To the north is the buffer zone housing the service areas: garage, workshop, entrance hall, and wood stove. While to the south the terrace and pergola form a large glazed facade, which forms a trombe wall. Finally, there are external fabric structures, and a water pool reflecting the sun's rays in front of the facade. Each of these spaces has a different level of comfort. The core is designed to house the family during the most severe weather conditions; a refuge. While the full house with its area of 270 square meters, spreads out into the garden space and can house a large family during good weather.

The proposed lifestyle could be referred to as nomadism. The inhabitant chooses his or her living conditions according to external climatic conditions. The house, including the supermonitory spaces around the center core has a traditional energy consumption. The occupant moves around within the home according to his space, comfort, and energy requirements as well as to his psychological or social needs. Rammed earth houses exploit to some extent this device. In front of each house is a south oriented terrace which naturally extends the living spaces on three levels. The roof consists of a translucent envelope forming a heat capturing solar collector from which warm air is extracted to the living spaces. The large overhang of this roof protects the walls consisting of compacted soil drawn from the site. The fabrication of these materials requires a low energy input, and is also totally recyclable. The three different materials of the three primary interconnecting elements: the greenhouse, the walls, and the terraces were chosen for their energy-capturing qualities.

This theory of volumes within volumes was also exploited in the building of a school in Cergi Pontois, a new town near Paris as part of the energy efficient school program. Commonly shared spaces of a school — play room and library — are inserted into the void defined by the classrooms: squares interlock with other squares. They therefore create

Gilles Perraudin
Jourda & Perraudin, Architects

13.04 the double collector facade to the studios at the School of Architecture, Lyon.

13.05 study model of the relationship between the undulating school building and the planted roof of the "Life Center": the International School in Lyon

charismatic volumes forming buffer zones. External spaces shelter it from the weather, and make it accessible to the pupils. The classroom, as well as the central communal spaces face onto this passive space, and therefore have no direct relation with the exterior. In this case the system of encasement follows an internal order.

In the building for the school of architecture in Lyon, for which we won the competition in 1982, the principle of a buffer zone is demonstrated by the central streets carved into the massive base of the building. It is a non-heated space whose temperature is moderated by the heat lost from the teaching and service areas. The double facade of vestibule workshops, a totally glazed accessible volume, captures solar energy, collects warm air, and extracts it to other parts of the building, in particular by the transfer from one facade to another. In the same way, the large, semi-circular glazed hall of the administration block is a space of intermediary comfort towards which face the glazed facades of the office spaces. The internal skin of a double facade to a studio workshop is naturally ventilated by a series of opening panels: the design of which mark a premise for a more general conception of energy-capturing envelopes which adapt to their environment.

In the factory project fnear Munich, Germany, it is the production area that is included within the double envelope. A winter garden is formed between the double skins of the facade. Timber modules within this zone provide office and service spaces which are oriented both to the exterior and onto the factory floor. The roof is made of an external skin which forms a weatherproof layer, and an internal skin equipped with motorized adjustable panels. This internal skin is the element of a climatic control, closing and opening according to energy gains or demands. The composite roof covering also allows for the integration of solar water heaters and photovoltaic cells. The PV cells provide the energy required to reorient the roof configuration in order to optimize the solar energy gain. The energy calculations show a saving of about 30% on consumption.

This transformation of the envelope is not only day by day but even hour by hour according to the seasonal movements of the sun, and ambient temperature. This means that we can consider the building as a space enclosed by a continuously changing envelope, and not as a rigid volume with sealed enclosure that could be considered as forming an artificial environment divorced from nature. In the previous project there is a technical approach to the double skin roof. Whereas in the International School building in Lyon, the roof envelope responds not only to the climatic requirement, but also acts as a large shelter under which are found independent, both architecturally and structurally, buildings accommodating a variety of activities along a 120 meter

13.06 East elevation of the gymnasium and the suspended planted roof: the International School in Lyon.

13.07 the south facade with terrace, protected overhead by a textile canopy: house in Lyon-Vaise.

long internal suite, which is covered by a glazed roof.

This structure, covering 8,000 square meters, suspended from 17 masts, and on which is planted a grass field, covers and protects a village formed by the commonly shared spaces for the entire school. It creates an intermediary climate between the exterior and the interior. As in the school of architecture, temperatures are also moderated by the heat lost from the inner buildings. A buffer zone is formed between the interior protected spaces, and the exterior. This forms a space offered to the community, a public space. It unifies the whole space while permitting the diversity of form, and use of the inner building. A world apart is created both above and below ground. On one end, the massive planted roof; and the other light, the suspended roof. Opaque and transparent, internal and external, natural and artificial. These vast roofs, under which are housed the various common spaces for the school are connected to classroom buildings, whose layout assures constant protection from the northerly and westerly winds. The teaching building faces east over the planted field, while the northern and western facades which curve along the Rhone river enclose the buffer zone, which is also an intermediary climate. In this zone are found all of the circulation spaces, both vertical and horizontal, the play areas and service spaces.

This facade is openable, forming a relationship

between the galleries along which the pupils circulate, and the conference space at the meeting of the contrasting waters of the Rhone and Versonne rivers, which are two rivers crossing Lyon. The east facade is protected by solar shades, the angle of which has been calculated for each meter in length in order to assure an optimum control of daylighting. This theory of a continuous cover floating over living spaces is also to be found on a smaller scale in the projects for an experimental private house at Stuttgart, as well as in the private house in Lyon. In Stuttgart, the roof covers a house laid out like a Neapolitan slice. It's a name given in France to a dessert made up of slices of different flavored ice cream. It's because the house is layered in different zones. On the northern side of these houses, the roof curves down to the ground level, sheltering the entrance hall. A non-heated space which is simply protected from the weather. This roof continues above a stone house (minimal home) and the glass house which is extended at each level by the living spaces of a stone house. This roof, supported on inclined, treelike structures, becomes a louvered sun shade to the south, protecting the glass facade as well as the terraces, and the private gardens. This waterproof shelter considerably simplifies the construction process as the site is protected from early on in the project.

The private house in Lyon exploits this system more fully. Offering possibilities for extensions and

13.08 interior of house at Lyon-Vaise, with plywood panelling being used for the external facade, the floors, the walls and the ceiling

13.09 section drawing for the competition for the European Parliament building in Strasbourg.

transformations of the home under a tensile textile cover. This roof forms an umbrella during the construction phase. Protecting the assembly of the timber modules, made of insulated plywood, within which are housed the living spaces. The geometric form of the roof was calculated in order to maximize the penetration of the sun rays during the winter months through a single glass facade of 21 meters long, while in the summer, protecting the facade and external terraces. The treelike canopy complements the natural existing trees on the site. This theory has already allowed several extensions and modifications to the house, and in this way accommodates the changing lifestyle of a family.

This project led to the idea of a formalized freedom in which the architect is able to define the internal volumes under the same envelope according to different brief requirements. In this way, architectural contradictions can coexist due to the unification generated by the overall shelter concept. In the project for the Indira Gandhi National Arts Center in New Delhi — which was also a competition, in which we won the third prize — this shelter theory, independent of the inner buildings, is generalized and adapted to a tropical climate. The shelter, in this case, protects from the rain, but is open to the air. Air movement is reinforced by the use of the Venturi effect, which is complemented by an evaporative cooling system to reduce the ambient air temperature. Each building can be individually expressed

due to its independent structures. The roof could allow the center to exist even before the installation of the equipment. Symbolically this overall unity brings all the elements together, while each building can be varied in terms of materials, form, and structure, so expressing the diversity of cultures and languages of the Indian subcontinent.

The project for the European Parliament in Strasbourg, equally expresses on the one hand the necessity of the unification of the different cultures that constitute Europe, and on the other their diversity. A continuous envelope encloses all the offices, meeting, and conference rooms, exhibition spaces, and the Parliament debating chamber. Within this single volume is a protected microcity consisting of separate buildings, courtyards, gardens, and suites, connecting the different entities, and lit by roof glazing. The envelope opens up, closes, becomes opaque, translucent or transparent in order to adapt to the external climate. None of these spaces are oriented towards the exterior. They always face onto the intermediary spaces, the buffer zones. Garden spaces, meeting areas, and public places at the scale of this microcity. Thus the theory of the double envelope, the overall shelter, and of the intermediary public spaces were applied to a number of the open projects. During the competition for the Hotel du Departement in Bordeaux, the concept of the vertical city within its protecting envelope was explored. This unifying envelope, once again,

13.10 layers within layers of the microclimatic envelope: the Training Center in Herne-Sodingen, Germany

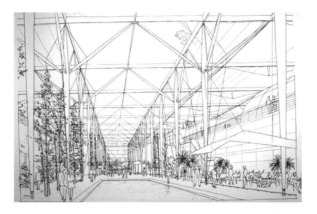

13.11 perspective of the interior of the glass house which forms a protected microclimate.

organizes the public spaces, that are at once both exterior and interior. They are stacked gardens from which large bays open onto the Mediterranean.

Finally it is the project for the training center for the Ministry of the Interior at North Rhine Westphalie in Germany that the concept of a microclimatic envelope is clearly demonstrated. Bringing together the different architectural theories that have been previously referred to. The hypothesis proposed by this concept is that an overall secondary envelope which encloses a volume surrounding independent buildings produce a number of environmental benefits. The inner buildings could be newly constructed or existing, and of diverse functions. The hypothesized benefits include: reduced energy consumption in enclosed buildings. The envelope acts as a thermal buffer zone in winter, and as a passive solar collector in the mid-season months. Protection of the inner buildings from wind in winter decreases effective U values of boundary layers, and simplifies the construction materials and method for enclosed building fabrics due to protection from external climate conditions. The transitional space between the envelope and the inner buildings provides a type of public space where indoor and outdoor activities can develop protected from direct external weather conditions. The principle of nomadism is induced with people moving in and out of the inner buildings as temperature permits. The hypothesis and the desired effect of the enve-

lope is illustrated by the metaphor of climatic shift. This envisages that North European temperate climate sites, when enclosed by the microclimatic envelope correspond to a climate and atmosphere at latitudes further south in Europe. And so reduce the energy demands of the inner buildings. The envelope is to react to the surrounding environment, exploiting solar energy gains in the winter and mid-season. In the summer months, solar shading, natural stack effect, ventilation, water, evaporation features, and vegetation will protect and cool the inner spaces. In summer, to avoid overheating, certain elements of the facades will be opened, and the glass house will be ventilated. The shade of the trees, and the refreshing effects of fountains will cool the space. In order to cool the interior buildings, fresh air will be drawn in by the emergency exit tunnels from shaded exterior zones. It is predicted that the envelope will introduce savings of about 21% in terms of annual heating energy, and 18% in terms of CO_2 production.

The glass envelope creates a large protected space, offering the possibility of enriched exterior public life, as within a winter garden. Ponds with water jets animate the space. Offices are treated naturally. Areas are planted with dry grasses and ground creepers. Pathways are made of gravel and the terraces in wood. Vegetation includes eucalyptus, mimosa, and oak trees.

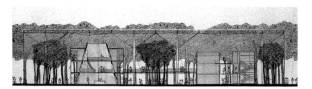

13.12 cross section showing the independance of the glass house structure from the timber building which it shelters: Training School at Herne-Sodingen.

The research conclusions of the project have been worked out with Ove Arup and Partners in London to assure the client that the concept is feasible. The results of this research project, which was funded through the European Commission, are summarized as follows. The climatic performance of the envelope, and its influence on the inner buildings are: the envelope acts as a climate-moderating device for European temperate climates, reducing the energy consumption of the inner buildings for heating and fresh air supply, saving 25 to 30% per year. Equivalent reduction in associated CO_2 of about 17 to 24%. Protection from wind in winter decreases effective U values of the inner buildings. Increased perception of comfort in winter, reduced wind chill factor, control of temperature within the envelope in summer by the use of a number of devices including natural stacked effect ventilation, solar shading, water evaporation cooling, and vegetation. These can limit temperature to a maximum of 2 degrees centigrade greater than external temperature in the central and least ventilated areas, and to an equivalent of external temperature in the perimeter zones. The risk of condensation can be minimized by draining the water basin in the winter. And depending on the ventilation strategy, this could be reduced to approximately 15 grams per square meter of water per day on some winter days.

Conclusion: the results demonstrate the feasibility a of microclimatic envelope from the point of view of the energy consumption. The building offers the possibility of new lifestyles for the users of the enclosed buildings, and the envelope thanks to the 176,000 square meters of interior protected space available. It especially offers a real alternative to the

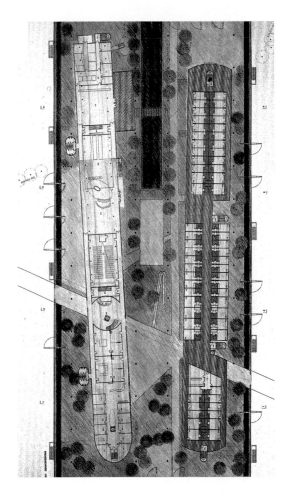

13.13 ground floor plan of the two buildings: the accomodation and the academy benefit from the micro-climate formed by the glasshouse.

functional, technical, and economic point of view to climatically controlled atriums, shopping malls, exhibition space, or tropical greenhouses which only accentuate the rupture with the surrounding environment. The microclimatic envelope reacts to internal and external conditions. It opens up and closes. It remains in close contact with the external environment due to its transparency, and its role as an intermediary climatic space, both functionally and socially.

14.00 model of the Shanghai Armoury Tower, designed with
Norindar Hamzah and Yeang International.

The Skyscraper, Bioclimatically Considered

Ken Yeang
T.R. Hamzah & Yeang Architects
Kuala Lumpur, Malaysia

14.01 Ant and termite skycraper construction

I have been working with skyscrapers for the last fifteen years. One of the most distressing things I find when students come to work for me is that they weren't taught how to design skyscrapers at schools of architecture. Eventually I found out that most schools of architecture consider skyscrapers evil, and that they don't want to teach how to design tall buildings. But whether you see them as evil or not, whether they are seen as a clean or dirty job, somebody has to do it. So I thought "Well if somebody has to do it, I probably should do it."

What is a skyscraper? A skyscraper is essentially a building with a small footprint, small roof area, very tall facades. And what differentiates it from the conventional low rise and medium rise buildings is that it needs special engineering systems due to its height. There is an argument by the Cambridge University Land Use and Built Form Research Group that you can build high density medium rise buildings. I made a diagram to show, you know, why you can't make it work. If you take a site with a footprint of around 50%, then the plot ratio is one to two; you're already at a three storey building. And at one to six you're at a ten storey building. That assumes that your car parking is put somewhere else, or put underground. But at one to six if your car parking is put above ground then you probably have something like a sixteen storey building. So what it means is that anything above a plot ratio of one to five, or one to six, becomes a high rise building straight away. In Asia now we are talking about plot ratios like one to ten, one to twelve, then the whole proposition of a high density medium rise doesn't work. And so like it or not, the high rise isn't going to go away. It's going to be with us, and somebody's got to do it; and we've all got to do it well.

It's projected that in the year 2000, more than 70-75% of North America's population will be in cities. So you will encounter the same problem with skyscrapers that we will have in the Far East, and schools of architecture will have to decide somewhere along the line that they have to teach students how to design tall buildings, and to approach it in some sort of meaningful way.

I started to look around and I asked myself "What are my friends doing?" What I found is that most of them are building what I call multi-storey refrigerators. Thick walls that don't have relationships between the inside and the outside. Now I started to work on ecological design about 20-25 years ago. And essentially, the principle of ecological design is that for every action of construction, you have four levels of impacts on the environment. Impacts of inputs, impacts of outputs, impacts of the system environment, impacts on the environment itself on the system. You find that 40% of the raw materials by weight are used in building construction globally each year, and 36-45% of a nation's energy output is used in buildings. And for building outputs, 20-26%

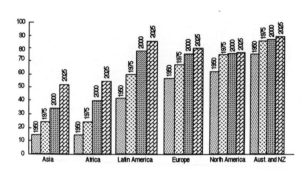

14.02 Percentage of population in urban areas, 1950-75, with projections to 2000-25.

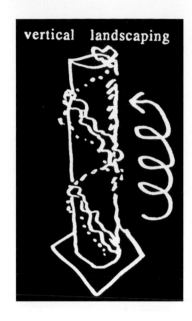

vertical landscaping

14.03 Ken Yeang's sketch of the idea of the vertically landscaped skyscraper.

of landfill trash is from construction, and 100% of energy used in buildings is lost in the environment. Architects actually have a significant contribution to make towards betterment of the environment, and towards a more ecological future.

I summarize ecological design into three basic sets of strategies. You don't have to do them all at the same time, but preferably you should do them all eventually. The first strategy is one I call design for efficient operations costs. That means efficient energy, materials, efficiency by design configuration by passive means with low environmental impact. Second level is design for efficient first costs. That means the energy, equipment and assembly that gives you efficient first costs with low environmental impact. And eventually if we have sufficient data to do this, we should design for efficient end cost and end use. That means the energy, materials, efficiency in the entire flow cycle from source to recycling and reuse is thought through by the architect and with low environmental impact.

Lets look at the first strategy you should use. If you look into the lifecycle of a built system you find that over 65% of its energy use is in the system operational phase. And therefore the first level of attack, if you like, as a designer in designing a low energy building is to look into how to reduce its energy use during its operational phase. Now what I've done is to prepare, if you like, a list of my design agenda for

designing the low energy tall building. The first one is what I call optimum use of ambient energy by using bioclimatic responses. The bioclimatic principle is basically very simple. If you're in Antarctica, you probably have to wear very thick clothes, and build thick houses, or big thick buildings with insulated walls. And if you're in Papua New Guinea you probably have to dress in a sort of light way, and in the tropics you have to have sort of light buildings. And so that's essentially the principle of bioclimatic design. That if you're in a hot climate then you should dress (or do your buildings) to make yourself comfortable in relationship to the climate of the place, and in a cold climate or a temperate climate you should dress and do your buildings in a similar way.

Termites design skyscrapers. The first thing you start to note is that termites are actually better engineers than we are. They can do tall buildings, skyscrapers several thousand times their own height. Whereas we can build skyscrapers maybe three hundred times our own height. But the other thing you should note is that there are skyscrapers built by termites in different climatic zones. Termites and ants already know how to do bioclimatic skyscrapers. They know how to use pitched roofs, sun shading, and things like that.

The logic of bioclimatic design demands that the building configuration should follow the sun path. As

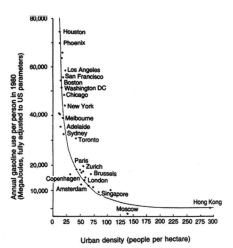

Gasoline consumption and urban densities (1980)

[Source: Paehlke, 1991]

14.04 the connection between gasoline usage and urban density in the major cities of the world.

14.05 Asia's first hairy landscaped tall building: the Menara Boustead building, Kuala Lumpur.

you go further away from the equator the sun during wintertime becomes more important. And as you go towards the equator, cross ventilation becomes even more important. One of the strategies you can use in designing a bioclimatic skyscraper is to use the elevator and the stair cores as solar and wind buffers. In a building that we are working on in Ho Chi Minh City the cores are on the east and the west sides. Incidentally, the building is at the end of a boulevard, and Ho Chi Minh City was designed by the French with boulevards and avenues. So what we have is a series of glass elevators with trellises all the way around. So the building is seen as a boulevard in the sky.

There are three basic ways of locating the cores in a tall building. You can either put them in the middle or the ends, or put it all to one side depending on the fire escape distance, about 15 meters from the furthest corner in most countries in the world. Locating the cores on the outside, on the east and west side of the building enables you to have natural ventilation and sunlight to the lift lobby, staircase, toilets, and escape stair. So that by putting the peripheral core on the outside of the building you have a cheaper building to begin with. You have no pressurization duct, so you have lower first costs, lower operating costs. You get up, you have a view out; you have an awareness of place. That means when you get up in a lift, you look out, you can see out of the window, and say "Oh here we are. We're

in Boston, or we're in Babylon." You know where you are and then you have natural ventilation and sunlight which is a healthier building to be in. And they're safer in the event of total power failure. That means, for instance when the bomb went off in the World Trade Center it destroyed not just the power supply but also the emergency generator. And so people tripped over themselves to find the lift core, which is in the middle of the building, and then tripped over each other trying to get to the ground floor. But if the core is on the periphery of the building, then once they found the core, the natural sunlight and ventilation will help them down.

We finished a building in Kuala Lumpur in 1985 and we put planting on the side of the building. When it was completed it was called Asia's first hairy building due to the terraces and the planting on the facade. The planters have a gravity fed sprinkler system that feeds water and fertilizers into the building, into the planters, so it's like a living organism in the middle of the town.

Kuala Lumpur is about 2.9 degrees above the equator, so sunrise and sunset are almost east and west. The building is designed with the cores on the east and west sides. What happens if you have a core on the North and South, and a core in the middle? I have taken an index, which is called OTTV. OTTV stands for Overall Thermal Transmission Value. It's not a very precise index,

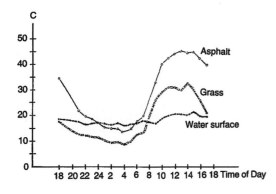

Surface temperature of materials

[Source: Meiss, 1979]

14.06 the rise in surface temperature of urban surfaces as the day progresses.

14.07 physical model showing sunshaded elevation of the Menara Gamuda building.

but I use it as a common index to evaluate the OTTV value for three possible configurations. Then you calculate OTTV for different facades, north, south, east, and west, and you total it. And the OTTV, if the core is in the middle is 51.57 watts per square meter. If it's north and south, it's 32.89. And if it's east and west it's 30.49 which is 40% less than what happens in the middle. So this is to demonstrate that just by locating the core you immediately have a passive low energy tall building without doing much else. Next is to try to use the sky courts terraces and balconies as places in the sky, or as inside/outside places, and as a transition space for bioclimatic responses.

Studies have focused upon what would you like to control if you had the choice? What would you like to control? A study carried out by a management company questioned about two or three thousand users "Would you like to control the lighting level? Would you like to control daylight, air movement, heating, cooling, temperature, noise distraction, furniture arrangement, air freshness?" There were three choices: no control; very little control; some control. An overwhelming 60% said they would like to control air freshness. Now it doesn't mean that as soon as you walk into a floor space you're going to leap off and open a window. But the whole idea that you can open a window contributes towards the occupant's wellbeing. And also you find that for indoor quality, 56% of poor indoor quality is due to

poor ventilation. What we do is to design a floor plan with windows all around, sky courts with an atrium above and sliding doors to act as filters to control natural ventilation.

When people move into an office the first thing they do will be to put all the partitioned offices around the outside. And so once you do this, the majority of the people who use the work stations don't get access to windows. So we tell the owners "Do the opposite. Put all the partitioned offices in the middle, and put everybody on the outside." Over 70% of the work stations get access to the windows and to sunlight. All offices will have full height glass so they can see out, and get access to a window. So in this way we shape the floor plate to adapt to inhabitants, patterns of views, for greater access to natural ventilation and sunlight.

The next thing is to try to recreate, if you like, some of the conditions on the ground in the air. And so what we want to do is to introduce vertical landscaping, and more importantly increase the overall organic mass on a site because the building is nothing more than intensive concentration of inorganic mass onto a small footprint. So what I like to do is to put as much planting as possible into the building. One way that I thought at the time was to try to use trellises to try to bring planting up in a continuous way. Studies have shown that 8% cooling load savings can be achieved from a 10% increase

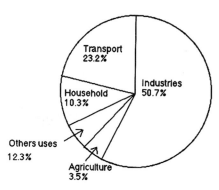

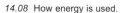

National Energy Consumption by Sector
[Source: Raju, M.K. (1996)]

14.08 How energy is used.

Ken Yeang
T.R. Hamzah & Yeang Architects

14.09 the skycourts, terraces, protective balconies and wind-scoops of the Menara Mesiniaga, Selangor, Malaysia

in vegetative areas; these are some of the benefits of landscaping. William McDonough talks about the building as a tree — I like the idea of that, in fact plants are located in a spiraling fashion around the facade of the building in Kuala Lumpur. We try to have continuous vegetation going up as much as possible. This will significantly contribute towards the greening of the environment if a skyscraper has a plant ratio of one to seven, then the facade area is equivalent to almost three times the site area. So if you cover, let's say, even two-thirds of the facade you've already contributed towards doubling the extent of vegetation on the site. So in fact a skyscraper can become green. And if you green it, you're actually increasing the organic mass on the site.

You have to decide exactly what natural vegetation is for. If it is for health you are talking about the rate of air change. For comfort it is the rate of air flow. For energy conservation it is about external wind speed. We have a building under construction now in Penang. What we tried to do is bring wind into the inner parts of the building. But it was a building that we designed for natural ventilation by default rather than by design because the client said to us "Well with the previous building, how much was it per square foot?" and I said "About $136." Then he said "Well could you do it for $110?" So I said "For $110, I'd have to take out the air conditioning. Then the tenants would put air conditioning in themselves."

So he said "Fine, take out the air conditioning." Then he came back and said "Well could you do it for $100 a square foot?" So I said "For $100 a square foot I'll have to take out the windows." And he said "No, no keep the windows, keep the air conditioning out." So we kept the windows. As you know, wind speed differ in different terrains. For a building of about maybe 17, 18 stories, the highest wind gust at the top is probably around 30 to 40 meters per second. Which is actually a very high wind speed. What we have are "wind shells". I call them wind wing walls. Wind wing walls generate the wind into the inner parts of the building. I have a shallow plan so that the executive's office can be in the middle, and no desk can be more than 6.5 meters away from the window. Remember that the wind speeds are different at different heights of the building. We have to break the natural ventilation of the building down into three systems at different heights. So at any time of the day if the external wind speed is say 3 meters per second, and the windows on that facade are 50% open, then on a northwest facade you get an air change of 10 air changes per hour. Now this looks interesting, but what it means is that if you want a naturally ventilated building you'll be leaping around adjusting windows, getting the wind speeds right. The whole idea of a naturally ventilated tall building can be successful if you're prepared to accept the fact that you have to have an inconsistent temperature and comfort level, and that you have to stop work occasionally to adjust the opening of the

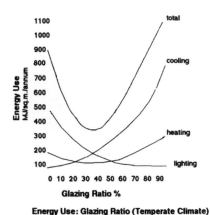

Energy Use: Glazing Ratio (Temperate Climate)
(Robertson, 6., 1992)

14.10 the impact of different levels of glazing in a facade upon energy consumption as expressed through heating, cooling and lighting.

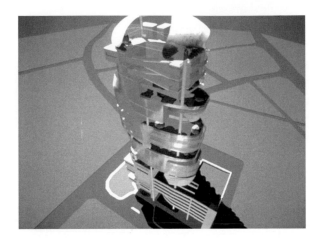

14.11 urban design in the sky: roofgardens, skycourts, solar shields and ramps articulated in the bioclimatic skyscraper: Hitechniaga Tower, Kuala Lumpur.

windows to get the wind correct.

Now at the same time we started to look at the sky-scraper like a city in the sky. We said "If you look at the intensiveness of the skyscraper at a plot ratio of maybe one to seven, one to eight, then a building would probably occupy, if it's a single story building, six blocks of New York." So if you think about the amount of area that you cover, then you have to see a skyscraper as a city, and you start to develop methods in which we could map the skyscraper in the same way that you map a city in terms of land use, density, population, community spaces, open spaces. We started to analyze the building in this way, and we found that instead of just evaluating the building, we could also inform ourselves on how to improve our design. For instance, we have dia-grams that show us the population density at different levels of the floors. For floors which have high partition density we should obviously increase the toilets, increase the public areas, increase the communal spaces, and linkages, and walkways. And of course, if you're working in different climatic zones, then you have the hot seasons and the cold seasons to deal with, and you have the two mid-sea-sons. So you have to design the enclosure, the skin as a responsive environmental filter for energy effi-ciency.

Of course, what we need to do is to design a sky-scraper more like a city in the sky, and recreate the

ground conditions. What happens if you want to move between floors? We need to look at a sky-scraper like an ideal city, and pick up all the things that you think your ideal city should be, and design the skyscraper that way. The ideal city should have good pedestrian linkages, should have public ground spaces, should be comfortable, accessible, commu-nity meaningful, should have shared service and variety, a sense of place.

What happens if you applied ecological concepts to urban design? Again, this is an area that we're work-ing on. The first thing we need to do is to adopt the ecological values planning method that Professor McHarg speaks of, so the development is in areas of low environment impact. You try and pick up areas suitable for development, and identify areas which are not suitable for development so that you don't build on these sensitive areas. Urban design must also resolve the need for transportation and its resul-tant relationship to a nation's energy use, as well as understanding the impact that surface materials have on ambient temperatures and the accumulation of energy. Reduce asphalt but increase water and grass.

What we need to do now is look at materials, look at the way energy is embodied in materials from very high energy, to high energy, to medium energy, to low energy. Different energy values for the material combined with strategies for the life cycle of the building. Do we reuse, recycle, or find a downgraded use? For instance — concrete, you can't reuse concrete as concrete, as at the end of its useful life it becomes landfill. You also have to look into the different ways you can construct the material into the building to enable it to be easily recycled or reused. I believe design should offer visions of better places, and address issues that will affect the user's future through bioclimatic design strategies.

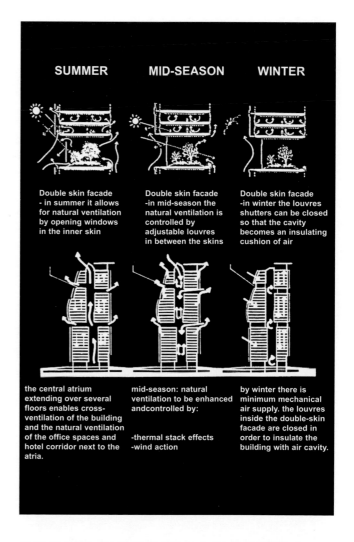

SUMMER   **MID-SEASON**   **WINTER**

Double skin facade
- in summer it allows
for natural ventilation
by opening windows
in the inner skin

Double skin facade
-in mid-season the
natural ventilation is
controlled by
adjustable louvres
in between the skins

Double skin facade
-in winter the louvres
shutters can be closed
so that the cavity
becomes an insulating
cushion of air

the central atrium
extending over several
floors enables cross-
ventilation of the building
and the natural ventilation
of the office spaces and
hotel corridor next to the
atria.

mid-season: natural
ventilation to be enhanced
andcontrolled by:

-thermal stack effects
-wind action

by winter there is
minimum mechanical
air supply. the louvres
inside the double-skin
facade are closed in
order to insulate the
building with air cavity.

14.12 the bioclimatic rationale in diagrams for the Shanghai Armoury Tower.

Spencer de Grey
Foster & Partners, Architects

Ecology in Architecture

Spencer de Grey
Foster and Partners, Architects
London, England

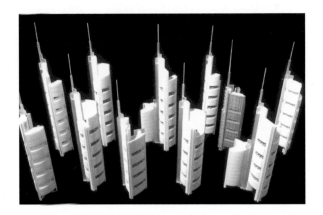

15.01 skyscraper model prototypes. Commerzbank, Frankfurt

I think that energy and sustainability is a crucial issue today for all of us. But it would be a great mistake thinking that it was an end in itself. It can only be part of a total picture which links a whole range of issues: urbanism, planning, the function of a building, what it actually looks like, and what it's actually like to use, and how people respond to the buildings. The crucial issue that we all face is trying to get that balance and the priorities right. It's quite fascinating when you look back at the United Kingdom since the Second World War. First there was a sort of active rehabilitation. We were obsessed with planning, and everything that went with it in a rather cold, mechanical way. Then as a complete opposite to that we became fascinated by style, and there was a battle of modernism versus postmodernism. I believe now that we're actually getting back to a more balanced overview. Which is very healthy. And I think architecture in the UK at the moment is in a very strong form.

A purpose of the Symposium was talk about energy, and its relationship to design. The issue of energy is important to architecture for it represents about 50% of the total energy used throughout the world.   How important it is that we control, and monitor, and design sensibly for the use of energy. Because 25% of the world is using 75% of the energy. So we owe it to the world, to take a very thorough, and analytical look at the way in which we use energy. We see all forms of diagrams and charts with all sorts of varying

figures. I think it would be wonderful if MIT took it upon itself to actually rationalize all those figures so that we are all discussing roughly the same numbers.

I think energy has always been at the root of all the buildings that we have designed. This goes back 25 years to the Willis Faber and Dumas insurance building in Ipswich. Here we were looking at a very complicated, difficult-shaped site in the middle of a historic town center. There was a strong urban issue here relating to the height of the building. Traditionally at that time it might easily have been a high rise, but in fact it was developed as a building that reached out to the perimeter of the site, and was just a mere three stories high. As one can see from reflections in it, it's very similar in height to the surrounding buildings. It was also very energy efficient. It had a very low external wall to floor ratio, a deep plan building where the energy costs were obviously carefully controlled. And that was made possible with the introduction of the atrium space at the heart, which was the visual and social focus of the two principal office floors on the first and second level. Then as you move to the top of the building, the extensive grass-turf garden, landscape roof. Again we provided a very high degree of insulation that had the added benefit of providing a very pleasant environment for the workers and staff in the building.

15.02 suspended glass wall. Willis Faber and Dumas building, Ipswich

15.03 natural lighting at the terminal building, Stansted Airport

That interest in the whole issue of energy conservation continued through into the third London airport, the terminal at Stansted. With the use of extensive natural light, and a very high performance external skin, we were able to completely alter the traditional expenditure on energy compared with other British terminal buildings. But of course it was the quality of natural light in particular that I think gives that building its very particular atmosphere and ambience as you move through it. It has proven to be a very popular terminal building for passengers. The traditional way in which terminal buildings are normally designed was with all the plant on the roof, and a very heavy structure to support it. And in consequence, no ability to use natural light whatsoever. So literally by turning that diagram upside down, as we did at Stansted, we were able to achieve the use of natural light throughout, provide a very simple, straightforward servicing diagram for the building, with easy access to the plant, and a very sensible distribution system up into the main terminal and concourse area.

At Stansted, we did work with Claude Engel, the Washington-based lighting designer, to look at ways in which the light can be tempered to minimize the contrast between the surface of the dome that encloses the public concourse, and the roof lights themselves with the suspended foils directly beneath the triangular roof lights. In energy terms, we were able to improve on the external performance of the

building by about three times that normally required under our British building regulations and we achieved a building that was about half the cost to run when compared with a traditional terminal. In particular there were massive savings in the use of artificial lighting. The building is hardly ever artificially lit and uses natural light throughout the day.

The city of Duisburg in Germany is a small town that was dependent on the steel and coal industry that ran into serious decline in the '70s and '80s. To regenerate itself it looked at the introduction of the microelectronic industry as a new form of industry for the city, and we were asked to produce an overall master plan for an inner city center, which led to a group of three buildings. The first of those is the Telematic Center, a flagship building to show how the city could rework itself. In some ways, the external appearance of this has some similarities with Willis, Faber in Ipswich; a sheer glass wall. But it's actually a much more complicated story than that. The overall energy strategy is one where we use solar collectors on the roof, and we use the town's main gas supply to provide the other source of energy. The gas is turned into energy through a cogenerator producing the electricity for all the power and lighting requirements and also heat which, when linked with the solar collectors on the roof, transformed it into the cooling system through the absorption cooling machine, that cooling taking the form of a chilled water system in the ceiling (a chilled ceiling system).

15.04 triple layered skin at the Business Promotion Centre at Duisberg

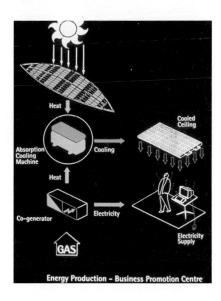

15.05 the principle of the energy system. Business Promotion Centre at Duisberg

The external wall is more elaborate, obviously, than the example some 20 years before it. It's a triple layer of skin. The outer single sheet of glass with the adjustable louvers in the major cavity, with a double glazed skin within. And that provides a very good performance external envelope; a thermal buffer between the inside and the outside. Then the chilled ceiling provides the cooling system, and the ventilation system (this is not an operable window building), being much smaller ducted fresh air direct into each floor at the window edge. With the return air being taken back in the corridor to be reused as part of the overall energy strategy. The ventilation system, when separated out from the full air conditioning system using air for the cooling, means that we have much smaller requirements in terms of depth for the ductwork. This in turn leads to a diminution of the floor to floor height, so that this building, when compared with a traditional air conditioned building, is much lower than it would be with the same floor to ceiling height. And that of course produces considerable cost benefit to the client.

Perhaps one of the most basic and simple buildings we've ever done is a high school for 900 children looking out over the Mediterranean in the South of France at Frejus. It's a long linear building two stories high. The inspiration for this came, obviously, from architecture on the other side of the Mediterranean where it gained the use of heavyweight construction; and good solar shading. The

basic diagram of the school is centered around a street which is the social center and the main circulation for the school, with two stories of classrooms on either side. The building is cross ventilated from the outside through the classrooms, and vented into that central street, then using the stack effect, hot air is exhausted naturally through the roof light, direct to the outside. Again, we use an exposed concrete structure throughout the entire building. There are no suspended ceilings whatsoever, and the concrete shells of the roof are separated from the waterproofing layer by a ventilated cavity to give an increased performance, keeping the concrete structure cool during the day whenever possible. Obviously, the shading of the south facade facing the Mediterranean is a crucial issue and so there are very strongly expressed blinds that pull out from the exterior face of the building to give shading both to the glass wall, and for people to be taught under. The detail of the very pronounced, fixed shading system does more than just shade the windows. It obviously provides ideal circumstances for the children to move out of doors when the weather is suitable.

The Electricity Board Building in Bordeaux is for a state run company and turned out to be one of the best clients I think the office has ever had. It was slightly disarming when we went to our first meeting with them having been appointed as architects, to hear that they were only interested in the appearance of the building, and they were in no way inter-

15.06 solar shading at the Albert Camus school in Frejus, France

15.07 elevational treatment at the offices of Electricite de France in Bordeaux

ested in energy conservation. After all, they were the Electricity Board of France, and burning energy was a crucial part of their daily wellbeing. So we didn't actually give up, and they actually turned into, as I say, an extraordinary client. We went back after the second meeting saying "Well I think you can have a building that looks very good, hopefully, but also it could have some very interesting energy concepts attached to it." And those ideas took root particularly with the local people in Bordeaux and Toulouse who were running the project; and it's now become a flagship project for the company to illustrate how electricity can be used sensibly and intelligently as part of an energy-saving strategy.

The building is very simple in its concept. The majority of it is office space. It's a regional headquarters for the Electricity Board. There is also a restaurant and entrance which split the building into two unequal halves; the majority being the office space. We explored the opportunity of providing very pronounced fixed solar shading along the two main elevations. The elevations face roughly east and west, but not exactly; and that led to two quite different shading diagrams for the two elevations to respond to that very particular orientation but using the same overall system. We used cedar wood as the material for the solar shading, which shades the majority of the elevation, but there's a very important zone, as in the previous Duisburg example, at the top of each of the floors where you get the translu-

cent material in the glazing to enhance the natural light bouncing back into the offices. We set the cedar wood shading against the brilliant blue of the shading system that lies behind. There are operable windows for all the offices so that you can get direct ventilation from the outside. Unfortunately, however, the building sits on a major road going into Bordeaux, so it isn't possible to open the windows all the time. So there is a backup system where natural ventilation comes into each of the offices through a sound attenuation system set at floor level with floor vents. That provides the basic ventilation rate for the building. The building, again, turns the traditional servicing system upside down. Everything is done from the floor level. There is a cast-in-place raised floor system into which we introduced microbore pipes for the cooling and for the heating when it's required in the winter, and that gives very good flexibility for the services. So the ceiling, again, is exposed concrete, and integrates the necessary artificial lighting. The exhaust air is taken out through the corridor, and recirculated in energy terms by means of a heat pump. In terms of its energy consumption, we are now monitoring, with the client EDF, the building during this coming year. We hope to come down to about between a third and a quarter of the energy consumption of a normal office building of this nature, and about half the rate of a good performance building. The results will be available in about six to nine months' time, and EDF are very keen, obviously, to have those results as part of their

15.08 the new Great Court at the redeveloped British Museum

Reichstag : Plenary Chamber : Natural ventilation and lighting concept

Exhaust air

Hot air

Natural diffused light

Fresh air intake

Air plenum
Air treatment

15.09 diagram illustrating the integration of natural light and ventilation at the Reichstag, Berlin

overall corporate strategy.

But the use of energy obviously doesn't only apply to new buildings. It is very important, I think, to look at the conversion or rehabilitation of existing buildings, and develop energy strategies for those buildings is equally, if not more, important. The British Museum, which attracts around 6.5 million people a year, compared with the Met in New York at about 4.7 million, is a very highly used building that was designed in the middle of the 19th century, and is now terribly overcrowded and desperately in need of more circulation space, more facilities within it. It's quite fascinating to see that when the building was originally designed, at the heart of the museum was a great garden. But unfortunately that garden lasted for only a couple of years, and you can now see in the middle of the courtyard at the heart of the museum the circular form with its dome of the round reading room, and all the book stacks that now cluster around it. Most of those bookstacks are built since the war. So there's an opportunity when the New British Library opens, and the British Library moves out of the British Museum building to look at that courtyard space, and in many ways to get back to the original diagram. So what we're proposing is to enclose that space, having taken the bookstacks down, to get back to the idea of a central space at the heart of the museum where people can move and be orientated, can eat, can buy things, and so on. We are able, which is very enjoyable, to pick up

on the natural ventilation system that was blocked off in the 1960s for the round reading room. The idea is for the new courtyard to use that basic ventilation system and to develop it further outwards so that we can actually naturally ventilate the whole of the courtyard, and exhaust that through the new roof. And in that way, we can develop a simple but energy efficient strategy for the great court. Obviously, the particular spaces within it like temporary exhibitions, and so on, would have their own environmental systems separate from that. But in principle, natural ventilation for the whole of the main circulation space.

Those ideas are taken much further in the proposals for the Reichstag Building in Berlin which was built at the end of the 19th century, and as everybody knows went through an extraordinary history. It's hardly ever been used as a center of government, and was left in a state of total devastation after the Second World War. There was a competition to select the architect. The first stage was quite interesting. They were looking for roughly three times the amount of accommodation that can be housed within the Reichstag. And our proposal at that stage was to build a very large podium and enclose both the Reichstag and that podium under a large umbrella roof, which obviously tempered the environment, and provided an environmental buffer between the outside, the Reichstag, and the lower podium area. At the second stage of the competition, the brief was completely rewritten, and the amount of accommoda-

15.10 old formal 19th century elevation of the Reichstag building, Berlin

15.11 new elevational model of the Reichstag for the new German Parliament, Berlin

tion was reduced to about a quarter of what was originally asked for. So we were able to get it completely within the existing Reichstag envelope. The strategy at that time, which has remained central to the strategies being built now, was to reopen all the courtyards that were part of the original design, which brought light and ventilation into all the spaces within the building. In the late '50s and early '60s the Reichstag had been completely remodelled. The courtyard spaces had been lost and a very heavy energy inefficient interior had been added. At the first stage of the design there was no visible external appearance of the new Reichstag emerging.

But on looking at the debating chamber, the concept of an enclosure that emerged out of the roof developed, that in some ways reflected the original dome that the building had when it was first built, but was actually doing very much more than just being a symbolic dome. It enabled us to magnify and amplify the whole natural lighting system for the debating chamber with the inverted conical shape of the reflectors that bounce natural light, and on some occasions sunlight, down into the debating chamber. The inside of it acts as a funnel for the exhaust air as part of the natural ventilation system and then, very importantly, the whole of the dome is a ramp for the public to go up to enjoy the views of Berlin. The whole of the roof being the public domain of the building. Obviously, when the sun is too great, there is then a sliding sun shade on a large scale that

comes across and blocks direct sunlight away from the reflector. We reactivate the natural ventilation system, a little bit like the British Museum, taking in natural ventilation into a lower air plenum beneath the debating chamber, that then percolates through into the debating chamber, and out through the inverted cone to the outside. The construction now is well under way, and we've now taken out all the '50s additions; which actually amounts to a very substantial amount of the interior.

The overall energy strategy is interesting. The project, when taken with a number of surrounding buildings, is big enough to justify it having its own powerhouse. We intend to burn rapeseed oil as the main fuel source and in energy terms, the Reichstag, with a number of surrounding buildings, will be self-sufficient.

Finally, to the Commerzbank in Frankfurt, a competition for a new headquarters that would work in conjunction with the existing building for around 900,000 square feet of office space with a further 500,000 square feet of other uses. The competition was a very fascinating one. There were ourselves, two Americans, and nine Germans competing for the project. The brief was very unusual, at least unusual to us when it was set in 1991, in that the whole strategy for the building was to be an ecological one where energy efficiency and natural ventilation were crucial words that threaded their way through the competi-

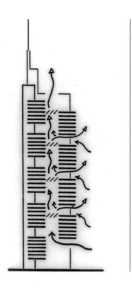

15.12 the idea of section. voids enable the flow of air and passage of light. Commerzbank, Frankfurt

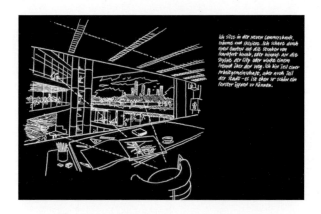

15.13 the view through the void to the garden and eventually to the City beyond. Commerzbank, Frankfurt

tion brief. The basic principle of the building is that at the heart of the building, instead of there being thick cores for the vertical movement of services there is a complete void that runs the full height of the building. And related to that void there is a sequence of gardens so that when someone is working on the inward facing offices they look across that void through the garden to the view of Frankfurt beyond. And those principles, which were established at the competition stage, are absolutely central to the building now that it is complete. The client was very interesting. It consisted of the Commerzbank, obviously, but also a key player in the whole development of the design was the City of Frankfurt, at that time run by the Green Party. They were very keen that this new building for the Commerz Bank reflected their Green philosophy and policies. One of those discussions was to do with the overall height of the building and various options which were placed in the city model to be studied with the bank and the chief planning officer. In the final design strategy we pulled in the expressed vertical movement that was previously on one corner of the triangular plan, and located it equally at the three corners of the triangle. So you get vertical movement at all three corners. That then leads to, obviously, three sides of the triangle; two of which are always offices, the third of which is always a garden. But the gardens don't stay fixed on one elevation, they rotate around the plan in such a way that all the offices are always in contact with one garden or

another. And particularly the inward facing offices with people working on the inner edge are looking across that triangular atrium through the garden to the outside. That overall form emerges in particular at the top of the building where the spiralling effect of the gardens is translated into the design at the top; with the top profile being staggered. We started off with twelve, three story gardens but felt unhappy about the proportion of that and so we ended up with a similar volume which has translated into nine, four story gardens. The point of the whole building. They will be very extensively landscaped with mature trees, and the planting will reflect, depending on the elevation, the vegetation of North America, Japan, or the Mediterranean. And it'll be here that you'll be able to come and have a coffee, have a snack, have your lunch as the focal point of four floors of office accommodation that relate to each garden. So really we're breaking the building down into a number of village units. There are 240 people who relate to each garden.

The garden is doing very much more than obviously being a social focus. It is also part of the whole natural ventilation system for the building. Obviously, you can open windows on the external face of the building, but we had to go through extensive computer modelling to see, and to prove to the German authorities, that the quality of fresh air inside the central atrium was good enough for natural ventilation. The natural ventilation comes in through the top of

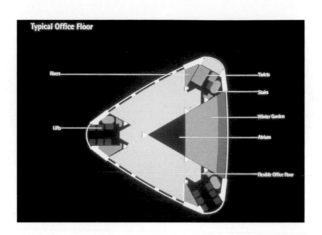

15.14 the building model photomontaged into the context. Commerzbank, Frankfurt

15.15 the principle of the 3 sided plan, with the garden rotating up the face of the building. Commerzbank, Frankfurt.

the gardens, and then moves up through the central atrium. And the atrium is subdivided into a number of twelve story units, i.e., three sets of four floors. And of course within twelve floors you get cross ventilation from the gardens in all three directions. We were able to show that the quality of air was more than adequate for all the internal offices to get their natural ventilation directly from the atrium. And of course that is further enhanced by the fact that that natural ventilation is passing through the greenery in the garden itself. So the quality of that air is very good.

Another key feature of the building is certain viewpoints around the city where you can actually get diagonal views right the way through the building. You see from one garden to another to the outside. So at certain viewpoints the building is semitransparent across its depth.

The structure is a steel structure, very unusual for Germany, and there are vertical masts that rise up either side of each of the three elevations. They support eight story steel verendeels that run that full height. That enables us to do two things: the gardens are completely devoid of any structure whatsoever, they're completely free space; and in the office floors there is no structure whatsoever actually on the office floor. Totally flexible office space which enhances the quality of space that's being produced inside this building.

The external facade allows natural ventilation for every office. People can open the inward facing flaps, but it is protected on the outside by a fixed pane of glass with the ventilation coming in through a bottom slot, and then being exhausted out of the top. When the conditions are too hot, too cold, or too windy, the building management system shuts the windows, and then a backup support ventilation system comes into operation, that is linked with the chilled ceiling system that runs through the ceiling throughout the building. But that chilled ceiling, again, only operates when the windows are shut.

The overall performance of the buildings in terms of its heating and cooling in both winter and summer shows the benefit of this strategy. We estimate that the natural ventilation system will operate on average for about 60% of the year, and 40% of the year will be too cold, or too hot, or too windy. With the automatic window system the ventilation system will be down to 35% of the traditional fully air conditioned office high rise building. So very substantial savings in energy are achieved.

Finally, it isn't just a question of an ecological high rise building, its setting in the urban context is a crucial consideration. Again, this results from work done with the chief planning officer. The concept is one of the tower rising out of the heart of the city block with partially retained and partially new perimeter buildings that relate the scale of the perimeter

Spencer de Grey
Foster & Partners, Architects

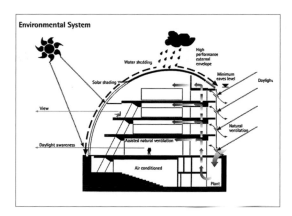

Environmental System

15.16 the environmental concept at the Faculty of Law building, University of Cambridge.

15.17 the 4 storey height stair, at the junction of the curved roof to the end glass wall. Faculty of Law, University of Cambridge.

edge of the site to the rest of this part of Frankfurt. There is an important square here from which one entrance is achieved, and then the main entrance to the tower is from the north on that elevation. The crucial gain for the city is a substantial enclosed winter garden at the base of the building that will be a public restaurant and public art gallery for the people of Frankfurt.

16.00   The Balcony by Edouard Manet (1832-83). Painted 1868-69.
© Photo RMN-Hervé Lewandowski.

Roger Stonehouse
University of Manchester

Dwelling with the Environment: The Creation of Sustainable Buildings and Sustaining Situations through the Layering of Building Form and Detail

Roger Stonehouse
University of Manchester
Manchester, England

16.01 the east side of Frank Lloyd Wright's Falling Water. completed 1937

We start with two observations.

First, in 20th century architecture we have seen a change from buildings with thick, solid walls with windows, usually small and nearly always openable, to buildings with thin, completely transparent (ideally visually non-existent) skins which have a completely sealed separation between the inside of the building and the outside. Here is a paradox; for the solid and thick is open(able) between inside and outside and the transparent and thin (with its connotations of supposed liberation) is sealed. In part this has been due to a change from selective to exclusive modes of environmental control*(1). But it is also symptomatic of a fundamental change in the way we see and experience the world; the way we are in the world. This change has its roots in Romanticism and the Picturesque when Man began to see himself as apart from nature, not a part of nature and consequently the environment; to see himself outside nature, looking on and viewing it to be both pleasured by its beauty and awed by its grandeur. There was also a similar dissociation from the cultural environment of history in the viewing of ruins and the creation of follys. It is not a big step from the viewing of the world through a Claude glass to viewing the silent world seen through a plate glass skin from the temperature and humidity controlled interior of Norman Foster's realisation of Mies van der Rohe's

glass skyscraper studies of 1919-21 at Willis Faber Dumas and, ultimately, to the virtual world viewed through a cathode ray tube.

Second, and conversely, over the the past two decades, the moves to make more sustainable buildings in order to reduce energy consumption and pollution through a return to selective modes of environmental control have generally involved not only a re-opening of the inside-outside relationship but also an increase in the sophistication of the layering of buildings between the inside and outside. We see such devices and elements as solar shading and screening, light shelves, balconies, reveals and shutters, and the use of thermal mass. Consequently there has been an increase in the real or apparent thickness of the wall and frequently a return to solidity and opaqueness pierced by windows, with the ensuing framing of view and modelling of light. Most significantly we see the reintroduction of degrees of enclosure at different scales at the edge of the building e.g. porches, arcades and conservatories and often deep into the building e.g. courtyards, atria, and galleria so that the building is seen as zones of differing degrees of enclosure which interact environmentally and may be inhabited and used differently in response to changes in the external environment. There has also been a reintroduction of openable windows and screens and blinds and shutters by

16.02 the translucent edge - Maison Dalsace ("Maison de Verre"), Pierre Chareau, 1932

16.03 the window which opens wide - solid yet open

Roger Stonehouse
University of Manchester

means of which individuals can manipulate their relationship to the outside world.

Two realisations flow from this second observation. First, as a result of the reopening and development of this relationship between the inside and the outside we have more opportunity to be aware of being in and a part of the environment. In part this is an argument for phenomenology and for physics; it is an argument for the living room which enhances the snowy day as analysed by Bachelard (2) with Frank Lloyd Wright's "fire burning deep in the masonry of the house itself" (3); for lying in bed on a hot sunny afternoon, the curtains swaying in the breeze, the dappled light, the sound of leaves rustling and distant voices and the scent of blossom through the window; for what Linda Heschong calls "thermal delight" (4); for the physics of heat and air flow expressed through and exploited by the forms of the buildings which are the places of our dwelling in the world, the situations of our lives. It is an argument for dwelling with rather than against the environment. The second and more particular realization is that it is precisely these situations at the edge, partially enclosed and partially open, which seem to be persistently attractive and enduring across all cultures, the back-to-the-wall (which is the built equivalent of the edge of the forest), the doorstep, the window sill on which to perch, the window seat, the balcony, the courtyard (which is the built equivalent of the clearing in the forest), the arcade, the porch, the belvedere. Various explanations for this persistence and popularity have been advanced, for these liminal and other situations, simultaneously inside and out, which seem to be so sustaining to our sense of wellbeing. They have been seen variously as reconciling us with the trauma of transition from birth to our development as individuals and the mediation of the individual with the universal, about which Colin St.J. Wilson has written so cogently (5) and as based in the satisfying security of the cave-prospect situation of prehistoric times (6), where the mouth of the cave might give both the opportunity for retreat to protective shelter and an elevated view of the distant approach of danger or potential food. Frank Lloyd Wright's houses have been revealingly analyzed by Grant Hildebrand (7) from this latter perspective, which may account for their persisting appeal.

It is no accident that in A Pattern Language (8) we find illustrations of examples of many of these persistently recurring and surviving situations for whilst this is not an argument for Pattern Language the connections are clear. In buildings designed for passive and inclusive means of environmental control we see many instances of the rediscovery, reworking, transformation and extension of traditional types and patterns of places and situations which are at the edge,

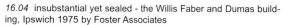

16.04 insubstantial yet sealed - the Willis Faber and Dumas building, Ipswich 1975 by Foster Associates

16.05 traditional mirador balcony in Cordoba, Spain

Roger Stonehouse
University of Manchester

simultaneously inside and out, or which bring the outside in or create degrees of enclosure outside; for this is an architecture of well known and half forgotten places, in which we may, in T.S.Eliot's words "arrive where we started and know the place for the first time". We see, for instance, developments of window reveals and shutters, window seats, balconies, awnings, bed cupboards, outdoor rooms, lobbies, conservatories, courtyards, atria, pergolas, porches, porticos, verandas, belvederes, galleria , hanging gardens, deep eaves and glazed and blanketing roofs. We see examples throughout this book and in the work of Jorn Utzon, Henning Larsen, Ralph Erskine, Glenn Murcutt, Charles Correa and Geoffrey Bawa and in such progenitors as Kahn and Wright (9) and they are deeply embedded in Palladio's reworking of the traditional farmhouses of the Veneto (10). These types and patterns are rooted in our experience of being-in-the-world, in the situations through which we begin to make sense of the world and our place in it; through their reuse and transformation they accumulate potential for meaning and in doing so the transmission of intended meaning, through convention, becomes possible.

But this layering of degrees of enclosure not only works environmentally, psychologically and phenomenologically it also underlies the way we structure our lives socially. This can be seen, for instance, in

sequences of spaces of increasing enclosure and privacy and/or status and in, for example, the porch; a place which is both public and private and consequently a place of transaction between public and private worlds. This structuring of our social lives through the layering of degrees of actual or implied enclosure occurs at all scales, for instance, the weather strip threshold - do we decide to cross it or not? At the urban scale where Richard MacCormac (11,12) argues for this layering to encourage and facilitate transactions, as he calls them, between inner private realms and the outer public urban realm, where the street market is a place of maximum transaction and the single occupancy, single entranced office block a place of minimum transaction. At the scale of the individual building Hillier and Hanson (13) in their adjacency graph analyses of plans have demonstrated the topological layering of buildings of different functions and of the same function at different times, showing how the layering is used as a form of control and as an expression of social power.

There is a reciprocal aspect to this layering of degrees of privacy at different scales, which, as we have seen, is also simultaneously the layering of the means of environmental control, for it also conditions the way we see and reveal the world and ourselves in the world and to the world. We see this, for

16.06 the adaptable nature of the facade - high density housing in Hong Kong

Roger Stonehouse
University of Manchester

instance, in the framing of windows and reveals (and here is an interesting ambiguity of words, for we frame a view of the world and reveal a picture of ourselves as perhaps we wish to be seen). The veiling of curtains of different degrees of opacity in an English living room, the finely pierced screen that is an Indian jalaka, and the stained glass screened balconies of Cordoba in Spain and the shutters of Italy tell us not just about climate but also about culture and their inter-relationship; they also tell us something of the sense people make of their world and their place in it. So we see this layering as also being essential to the way we can sustain and be sustained by our social and cultural relationships and understanding.

But having set up this argument for layering we can begin to go deeper, and here there is space just to raise the hem of the curtain, for we make sense of the world through inclusion and exclusion and of being inside or outside and our experience of this. For we are born, cradled, sit on a knee, sit at the doorstep, half in and half out, close to mother but daring to venture forth beyond the garden gate, and so on. We feel loved and included or disliked and rejected. In this way the experience of being in or out or between has become rooted in our values and culture. We see the world"'through a glass darkly". Who knows what happens "behind closed doors"?

Or what danger "lurks within","cloaked in shadows"? We counterpose urban (in) and rural (out); civic and barbaric; or now in a reversal of values, town (bad) and country (good). We are "cast out into the wilderness", out from that which is secure (secure in our knowledge), as were Adam and Eve. Good is seen within, evil is without and cast out to where it supposedly belongs, and so on.

But we can go even deeper beneath the world of meaning and value in unpeeling the onion of the argument, for this topology of inclusion and exclusion and overlapping underlies the way we structure our language, our thoughts and classification of the world and the mechanisms of perception in the Gestalt processes, ultimately the distinguishing of figure from ground; in distinguishing the self, by perceiving it as separate from the environment, which, in turn, is looked out on from within the self, as we struggle individually to make sense of that environment and of ourselves in the context of that environment.

So we may see the re-establishing of more richly layered relationships between inside and outside, which inevitably rediscover, extend and rework traditional types and patterns in a process of continuity and change, as essential to the creation of environments which are sustaining for individuals and societies and which are sustainable environmentally and

Dimensions of Sustainability

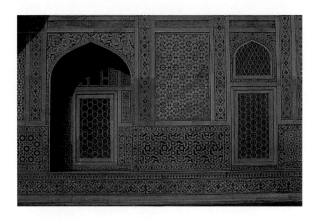

16.07 traditional jalaka elevatio, Agra, India

Roger Stonehouse
University of Manchester

culturally and enable us to dwell in and with rather than outside and against the environment.

* The selective mode "depends upon the selective admission of substantial elements of the external environment into the building" and the exclusive mode "uses the building envelope to exclude the effects of the external environment upon the interior conditions" which are (ideally) totally controlled by energy consuming servicing systems.

References.
1. HAWKES, D. The Environmental Tradition.
E &F N Spon
2. BACHELARD, G. The Poetics of Space Beacon
3. WRIGHT, F.L. Modern Architecture 1931
4. HESCHONG, L. Thermal Delight in Architecture.
MIT Press
5.WILSON, C.StJ. Architectural Reflections.
Butterworth
6. APPLETON, J. The Experience of Landscape.
John Wiley
7. HILDEBRAND, G. The Wright Space, University of Washington Press
8. ALEXANDER, C., ISHIKAWA, S., SILVERSTEIN, M.   A Pattern Languag. Open University Press.
9. BANHAM, R. The Architecture of the Well-tempered Environment. Architectural Press
10. KUBELIC, M. 'Palladio's Villas in the Tradition of the Veneto' p91-116. Assemblage, October 1986 MIT Press
11. MacCORMAC, R. 'Urban Reform' The Architects' Journal, 15 June 1983
12.MacCORMAC, R.   'Understanding Transactions'. The Architectural Review, March 1994
13. HILLIER, W. and HANSON, J. The Social Logic of Space. Cambridge University Press

Photographs: who's who?

Andrew Scott

William Mitchell

Ian McHarg

Bill Browning

Alan Short

Guy Battle

Christopher McCarthy

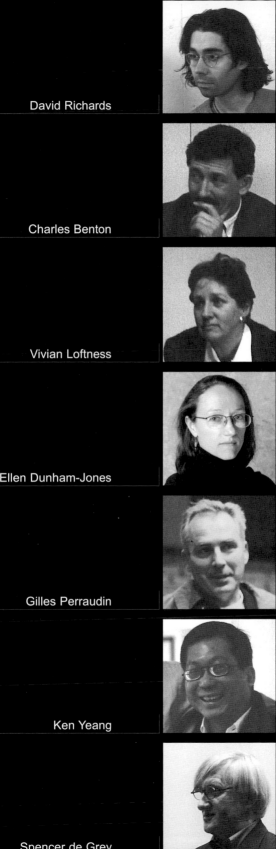

David Richards

Charles Benton

Vivian Loftness

Ellen Dunham-Jones

Gilles Perraudin

Ken Yeang

Spencer de Grey

Image Credits

While every reasonable effort has been made to trace copyright owners and credit the original source of images, it has not always been possible to do so. Certain images exist in the public domain, the use of which the editor is most grateful. Where known, the original place of publication for an image is also credited.

iii	Embracing Earth: NASA Apollo Mission
viii	unknown
x	Embracing Earth: Woiceshyn, Morton and Peteherych
2.01 - 2.02	The Prodigious Builders: Bernard Rudofsky
2.03	Architecture without Architects: Susumu Higuchi
2.04 - 2.08	Andrew Scott
2.09	Battle McCarthy
3.00a	Wired: Stephen Simpson/ FPG International
3.00b	Wired: David Turnely/ Black Star
3.01	Industrial Design: All rights reserved
3.02 - 3.09	William J. Mitchell
4.00	Embracing Earth: Lee Fu and Benjamin Holt, NASA/Jet Propulsion Laboratory
4.01	Design with Nature: American Museum of natural History
4.02	Design with Nature: After Sinott and Wilson, Nature: Earth - Plants - Animals
4.03	Design with Nature: Aero Service Division, Litton Indsutries
4.04 - 4.07	Ian McHarg
5.00	Architecture and Urbanism: Jan Derwig
5.01 - 5.06	William D. Browning, Rocky Mountain Institute
5.07	Jen Seal-Uncapher
5.08	Place Architects
5.09	unknown
5.10 - 5.13	William D. Browning, Rocky Mountain Institute
5.14 - 5.15	John A. Clark Compnay
5.16 - 5.17	The Inn of the Anasazi
6.00	Short and Associates
6.01	Peter Cook
6.02	Short and Associates
6.03 - 6.04	Peter Cook
6.05 - 6.09	Short and Associates
6.10 - 6.12	Peter Cook
6.13	Short and Associates
6.14 - 6.15	Peter Cook
6,16 - 6.17	Short and Associates
7.00 - 7.17	William McDonough and Partners
8.00 - 8.05	Battle McCarthy
8.06	William Alsop
8.07 - 8.17	Battle McCarthy

9.00	Ove Arup Partnership
9.01	Jack Pottle, Esto Photgraphics, Inc
9.02	Ove Arup Partnership
9.03	Murphy Jahn Architects
9.04 - 9.05	Ove Arup Partnership
9.06	Davis Brody Bond Architects and Planners
9.07	Jack Pottle, Esto Photgraphics, Inc
9.08	Ove Arup Partnership
9.09	Kiss and Cathcart Architects
9.10 - 9.13	Ove Arup Partnership
9.14	Esto Photgraphics, Inc
10.00	unknown
10.01	unknown
10.02	San Francisco Chronicle, 1993
10.03	Libby-Owens-Ford Glass Company
10.04	MCA Publishing
10.05-10.09	Charles Benton
10.10	Susan Ubbelohde
10.11	Harry N. Abrams, Inc
11.00 - 11.03	Vivian Loftness
11.04	DEGW
11.05 - 11.06	unknown
11.07 - 11.10	Vivian Loftness
12.00 - 12.01	Philip Jones
12.02	Douglas Kelbaugh
12.03	Nicholas Grimshaw and Partners
12.04	Douglas Kelbaugh
12.05 - 12.07	Ellen Dunham-Jones
13.00 - 13.14	Jourda and Perraudin Architects
14.00 - 14.12	T.R. Hamzah and Yeang Sdn. Bhd
15.00 - 15.17	Foster and Partners
16.00	Agence Photographique de la Réunion de Musées Nationaux, Paris. photo: Hervé Lewandowski
16.01	Dover Publications Inc. FLW's Fallingwater. photo:Harold Corsini
16.02	unknown
16.03	Pattern Language 236. Christopher Alexander. photo: Martin Hurlimann
16.04	Architectural Review 943. September 1975
16.05	Roger Stonehouse
16.06	Andrew Scott
16.07	A History of India, Christopher Tadgell. Longman Group UK Ltd 1990

Index